Dance of the Zodiac
How the Celestial Cycles Shape Your Physical Appearance

~~

This is the Revised/Enlarged Edition of the
2012 version of **Dance of the Zodiac**,
The Rhythms and Patterns of Creation

Published by Starry-Eyed Productions
www.astro-visions.com
1019 11th St., Lewiston, Idaho 83501

ISBN: 978-0-9614627-3-4
Library of Congress Catalog Card Number: 2021923995
© 2022 by William Schreib

~~

How this all began....

In 1974, my friends Larry and Gail Adams introduced me to astrology. This author respected their views, since they were the most well-read couple that I knew—and they had an amazing understanding of past and present history. I pretended to accept their ideas on astrology, but to be honest, I believed that astrology was nonsense!

Naturally, this tenacious Capricorn proceeded to prove to these two friends that astrology was a *bovine by-product*. I begin by gathering facial photos of friends and acquittances with Taurus Sun Signs. (Larry and my dad were Tauruses). A month or so later, I took the photo collection to their home—"to point out that the facial photos had nothing in common". Calmly, they pointed out the similarities in the features. Shall I say: "The rest is history".

Enticed by their comments, I found a book that described the mechanics of the Modes and Elements. They became the visual reference, that led to my renderings of the patterns of the Modes. When I added in the rhythmic force of the Elements, I was on my way to creating the 12 Zodiac caricatures that you will see in this book. Of course, the 1st Sun Sign to be completed was Taurus. Fourty-five+ years later, Gemini is still not complete, because every time I look at it, *I want to change it!*

Forward

This 2022 edition of "*Dance of the Zodiac*" is a revised and expanded version of the 2012 version. Twelve new pages of material were added, to provide additional insights into aspects, duads, body language and "How to Guess A Person's Unknown Ascendant". Many photos were updated and the text was rewritten to correct my errors, improve clarity and provide new insights.

In this book's 1st Edition, this author suggested that a person's character and appearance was determined by *the seasonal qualities at one's time of birth*. Since this author was raised in this northern half, I wrongly assumed that people born in the Southern Hemisphere were taking on the qualities and character of the opposite season. However, sometime after the publication of the 1st edition, I noticed that several Australian-born celebrities were showing the traits of their Sun Signs, but NOT showing the traits of their season of birth. With this, I asked Australian astrologer Santos Bonacci "Why do you show the traits of Aries and so little of the calmness of Libra?" I explained my interpretation. He chuckled—and then replied:

"The Sun's position (degree and Sign) on the ecliptic determines the Sign of the native in both hemispheres, North or South—and everyone who is born on the Earth in that month will have that Sun Sign, as the Ecliptic determines all things". He then added: *"Also, on **every location on the Earth**, every person born in the morning hours at sunrise will have that Sign Rising on the eastern horizon."*

With this, it became clear that this author's belief that our physical traits were a product of the seasons was incorrect, for all of the variations in the seasons* (and those in our human traits) are created by *the Sun's angle to the Earth's Equatorial plane—and our planet's powerful magnetic fields!*   *To see how this angle creates the 4 Seasons, go to pages 8 and 9.

It is the **Rising Sign** on the Eastern Horizon of the chart, that **defines the angle** between the *Sun's beams of light*—and where and how they overlap and intersect the magnetic lines on the different parts of the Earth. All the while, our solar system's other planets are also changing their angles to Earth's Equatorial Plane.

With this 2nd Edition's new additions, revisions and the updated facial images—this author believes that this book will provide the physical evidence, that will prove that astrology works!

William Schreib, 2022

Table of Contents (Page 1)

The Beginning of Astrology

The earliest astrological writings were seen in *The Vedas*—the ancient spiritual texts of the Hindus. Several thousand years later (around 2,500 BC), "tropical astrology" appeared in northern Africa. Both of these maintained that the placement and angles of heavenly objects were shaping the character of all life on our Earth. The westernized view was cemented around 350 BC, in Plato's *Timaeus*. His thesis speculated on how movement of objects in space shaped the physical world. In this work, he gives a geometric formation to each of astrology's Four Elements (fire, earth, air and water, and then shows how they can assemble themselves into a unified whole. He called these 5 formations the **Sacred Solids**. (These 5 Solids will be explored on page 5).

Plato's fifth and final geometric figure is the **Dodechedron**. These 72° angles (on each of its exterior points) create **twelve inverted pentagons**. Each pentagon points in the opposite direction of its neighbor, to create the sacred soccer ball. This design shows how "everything that appears above is mirrored below". It suggests how and why astrology works.

Before we get into those "astrological angles", let's look at some modern science concepts, that support the concepts that were established centuries ago in the language of Astrology!

It doesn't get any bigger than this?

Let's start with a *"Way-Out-There"* interpretation from Jean-Pierre Luminet of the Paris Observatory. In 2013, he concluded that the remaining waves of the "Big Bang" had arranged themselves into a 3 dimensional pattern, that resembles the dodecahedron.

Luminent contended that all things that exited on one face of this giant ball would immediately reenter on the other side of the sphere. With this, he declared that the Universe was finite! His idea was based on Einstein's 1905 **Quantum Entanglement** theory. It was confirmed in 2021, when digital photos revealed that objects (in opposite and distant points from each other in the heavens) were countering each other's spin, polarity and movement—instantly, at 10,000 times the speed of light! This entanglement of matter in inner and outer space makes a finite Universe feasible. It also supports the tenants of astrology.

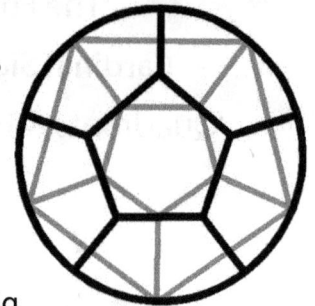

Let's bring this down to Earth:

In the mid-1980's, three Russian "Spiritual Anthropologists" (Goncharov, Morozov and Makarov) studied past cultures and surveyed the locations of over 4000 sacred sites, where pyramids, pagodas and the like were found. Without exception, every single surveyed site was placed near one of the lines on the Earth's global energetic grids. This showed that these lines were well understood and utilized by ancient civilizations.

Goncharov, Morozov and Makarov's Earth Grid

Technology reveals secrets of inner & outer space

In 1977, *Voyager 2* left the Earth's orbit to give us magnificent views of Saturn's rings and the hexagonal formation on its north pole.

In 1990, the *Hubble Space Telescope* began its capturing of distant points in space. For the first time, we saw the black holes in the center of galaxies and a multitude of once unseen galaxies and stars.

In the 21st Century, with the building of the *Hadron Collider* in the country of Switzerland, physicists peered in the other direction, to gain insights into sub-atomic structures and other quantum particles. There, quantum physicists unraveled the makeup of the smallest known "physical particles".

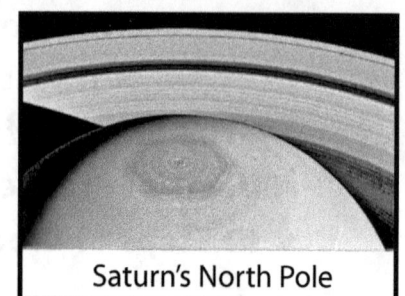

Saturn's North Pole

The mechanics of astrology appear in the smallest particles

Many insights into the smallest of particles were presented in the 2005 PBS Nova program *"The Ghost Particle"*. In that program, they demonstrated how the fusion of four hydrogen atoms into one helium atom creates the *smallest known units of mass*—**the Neutrino**. Each fusion creates two Neutrinos. With Einstein's E=mc2 formula, the missing hydrogen mass creates the massive energy of our Sun!

Each Neutrino is *10,000 times smaller than an electron* and over a hundred billion of them run through your thumb nail every second—nearly at the Speed-of-Light! They have *no electrical charge*. That is why this *"little neutral one"* is called a Neutrino.

This PBS program also showed how each Neutrino is made up of three different parts, that the physicists called "flavorings". This resembles the trilogy of actions, that are seen in astrology's **Three Modes**:

Flavor 1 (as illustrated in circle 1) sets the line of the beam on which light travels. In astrology, this is the **Cardinal Mode**—the highly directed force that initiates the creation of all things, big and small.

Flavor 2 defines the **Fixed Point**, or amplitude of the half-wave curve in the neutrino that appears, when light run slower than the speed of light.

Flavor 3 suggests the **Mutable** adjustments that will be needed, to weave the 3 flavors together, to structure the form of a Neutrino.

Note: Since the publication of the 1st edition of this book, physicists have discovered that sequential neutrinos create a "left and right hand spin" to each other. This spin places the 2nd neutrino in a reverse or flipped position to the 1st. Together, their alternation keeps all beams of light, on their forward track—to create the smallest waveform of harmonic resonant energies.

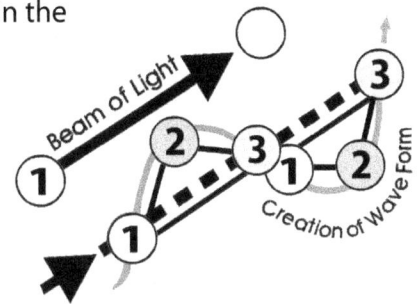

Astrology's 4 Forces & Elements are replicated in Quantum Physics

In 2013, scientists concluded that all particles were being formed by **Four Quantum Forces**. They called them the s*trong, gravity, electromagnetic* and *weak forces*. Appropriately, their names suggest the nature of astrology's **Four Elements**: The *strong Force* is the state of **Fire**, *the gravitational Force* is **Earth**, *the electric currents* are **Air,** and the *weak force* dissolves them all in the universal solvent of **Water.**

Later on, other physicists concluded that these four forces were each composed of smaller units, that they called **Quarks** and **Leptons**. True to the astrological principles, each force was generating three versions within itself. The *strong* and *electrical forces* create a set of **6 Quarks** that have the expansive/masculine qualities suggested in astrology's *Fire* and *Air* Elements. On the other end, the *gravitational* and *weak forces* were each producing **3 Leptons**, and the feminine-natured forces we see in astrology's *6 Earth* and *Water* Signs. In total, these *12 Quantum Particles* are similar to what we see in the makeup of the *12 Zodiac Signs*!

In the late 1960s, quantum physicists discovered that the character of all particles were being altered by the "vibrational qualities" of their neighbors. Soon, this *Bosonic String Theory* was expanded to include the gravity forces of planetary systems and galaxies. They called it the *Super-symmetry String Theory*. With that, let's toot our horn for the ancient astrologers—for they said the same thing, many centuries ago!

Quantum Entanglement confirms that the Universe is Unified

In the 21st Century, orbiting "digital telescopes" were giving us clearer photos of distant galaxies. In 2018, these images showed that the actions of distant objects were instantly altering the momentum, spin and polarization of other objects—at opposite points in space! All of this was occurring *at 10,000 times the speed of light!* This confirmed Einstein's theory of **Quantum Entanglement**. His theory supports astrology's premise that the *placements of heavenly objects* are altering the makeup of other distant objects in space.

Apparently, Einstein was not a believer, but his work supports the mechanics in astrology. In addition, there were many other scientists, humanists and magical tinkerers, whose work has provided fascinating insights into the tenants of astrology. Let's look at them, before we begin our "astrology lessons":

In between lies the Event Horizon

In between these largest and smallest of perspectives, lies the Event Horizon of "biological resolution".

In their research on *"The Resonance Project"*, physicists Nassim Haramein and Elizabeth Rauscher graphed resonant frequencies from the smallest to the largest known objects. These authors maintain that everything appears to be uniformly expanding and contracting in rhythmic, mathematical patterns. Their outward and inward arrangements always followed a miraculous linear progression on a graph.

Haramein and Rauscher concluded that our own living cells are the point where the micro and the macro join. **Life is the exact center** between these macro and micro extensions. Every individual is standing on your own "Event Horizon", experiencing the activities above and below. Their Resonance Project concluded that the angles between the parts (at both ends) were consistently changing the moods, attitudes and physical activity in each individual. All of life appeared to be affected by the angles in inner and outer space.

Thoughts Alter the Shape of Form

In Masaru Emoto's book *"The Message From Water"*, the interactive effects of environments, sounds and thoughts were brilliantly captured in his photographs of water crystals. Each droplet of water was frozen, as it was being subjected to an array of "orchestrated conditions". The results were amazing!

Classical music created beautiful symmetrical arrays of crystalline forms. Heavy Metal music twisted the crystals into fractured forms. Pollution and "thoughts of hate" distorted the structures into ugly formations. Emoto's photo evidence supports the idea that the vibrational nature of our surroundings—and our thoughts and feelings—are altering the shape of all things to come, in the future ahead.

▲ Thoughts of LOVE

▲ Thoughts of HATE

Life Adapts to the Changes

In the Nova program *"Ghosts in Your Genes"*, they showed how the horrid experiences of World War 2 survivors altered the genetic switches in their DNA, and how these altered genes were passed on to future generations. In contrast, they also discovered how diet changes and the presence of a caring "substitute mother" positively altered the DNA programming in diabetic mice. This shows how Genes adapt to different environments, by altering the biological information, that constructs all living organisms.

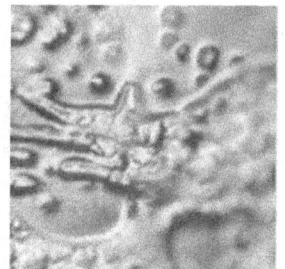

Each genetic unit is made of four chemically distinct nucleotides. They're linked together in chains of hundreds and up to millions of units of DNA. **Each chain contains a series of switches**—*that are altered by their surrounding conditions.* Most genealogists believe that these "adaptive switches" are how the many species of life learned to survive—in the various environments on Earth.

Do Heavenly Arrangements Alter Genetic Switches?

If individual experiences alter genes, just imagine the effect of the arrangements, that are created by the Sun's angle to the Earth—and its powerful magnetic field! As hinted at in the Forward, the daily transitions from day to night may set off a different set of epigenetic switches. Perhaps that is why individuals, who are born at night, often show the nature of their Moons, more so than the qualities of their Suns.

With the completion of this overview, it is time to examine the previously mentioned **Sacred Solids** and show how their shapes create an increasing array of complex formations—from the smallest of particles to the arrangements in the heavens above. These Sacred Shapes became the foundation of astrology and they also revealed how everything is connected to *The Source*, that creates all things in the Universe.

The Sacred Solids define the building blocks of astrology

Previously, Plato's five 3 Dimensional Sacred Solids were briefly discussed. Here, they are examined in more detail, as we show how the first four of these geometric arrangements fill the "Void of Space" with physical patterns, that suggest the state and structure of astrology's **Four Elements:**

The first building block in the Sacred Solids is the 3-D triangle. Plato called it the **Tetrahedron.** This three-legged structure represents the initiating act of triplicity, that shapes all light into physical states of being! This is the spiritual force found in the **Element of FIRE.**

When 2 pyramids are placed together, with their peaks joined in the center, the 8 outer points form the four cubical faces of the **Hexahedron.** This construction represents the **Element of Earth.**

In the **Octahedron**, 2 pyramids are symmetrically joined at the base. Its 6 points and 8 surfaces create the form of a diamond. These points disperse the force in six directions. This form represents the **Element of AIR.**

When 20 equilateral triangles are joined together, they form the 20 facets on the **Icosahedron** crystal. This lacing of the 30 edges of these triangles suggests the multi-dimensional connectivity, that we see in the **Element of WATER!**

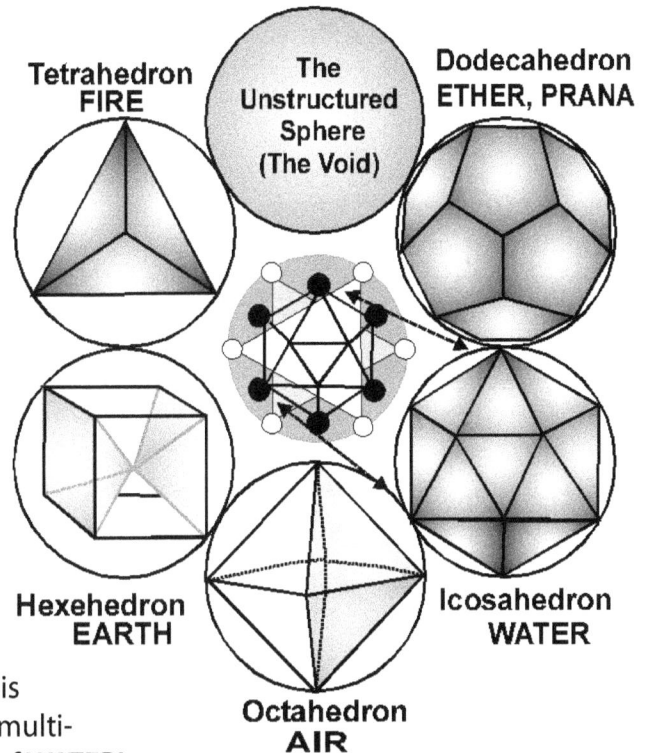

The final **Sacred Solid** is the *Dodecahedron*. This arrangement is not an Element, for Plato and many of the priests of his time, believed that this structure represented the all-encompassing essence of **Ether**. Others also call it called **Prana**. It was they considered to be *The Working Force of God*.

As astrophysicist Jean-Pierre Luminet postulated, this soccer ball (with its 12 pentagonal surfaces) is "the shape of the Universe". This combo of pentagon and hexagon facets creates what many call **a buckyball.** It was named after *Buckminster Fuller (born July 12, 1895),* the man who patented the geodesic dome.

Some contemporary physicists suggest that this combination of pentagon and hexagons defines the "Hyper-Dimension", where the Three Dimensions of Space merge with the Fourth Dimension of Time. Readers are not expected to understand all of this—it just confirms that today's scientists are saying what astrologers observed centuries ago, but in a more visual way.

The Shape of All Things to Come

Visually, the building of these Sacred Solids parallels what happens, when another electron and proton is added to the Element of Hydrogen. In the 1980s, Professor Robert Moon at the University of Chicago demonstrated how the entire Periodic Table of Elements—i.e., the building blocks of everything in the physical world—is created from various compilations of these 5 Platonic formations.

In this limited space, it is impossible to describe how these four elemental forms can be constructed into a dodecahedron. Any readers, who have that curiosity must watch **Frank Chester**'s video. In his YouTube video, he assembles an array of 3-D wire frames into a working dodecahedron.

With the completion of this overview, our astrological lessons begin, as we examine how the ancient stargazers were able to recognize how the angles between heavenly objects shaped the character and physical appearance of their friends and families.

The angles between heavenly objects define the geometry

Astrology's origins began as the ancients watched the Sun's daily movement above the horizon, its rise to high noon and its drop into Sunset and darkness. In the daily solar cycle, they saw that twelve groups of stars were regularly appearing on the eastern horizon everyday. With their observation of the seasonal changes (and the Sun's return to an established point in the sky), they determined that the year was around 360 days long. These insights gave humanity its 24 hour clocks and 360° circles.

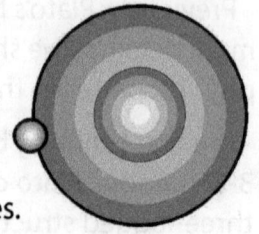

With this 360° circle, these ancient stargazers began the process of recording the angles between the transiting objects in the sky. As they watched, they found that certain angles would accelerate or restrain the timing or frequency of certain events. To capture these "up and down patterns", these brilliant astrologers alternately assigned feminine and masculine polarities to each of the 30 degree points in their charts.

The astrology chart clocks the daily and yearly cycles in the sky. Each of the twelve divisions represent two hours in the day, while each of the chart's 90 degree quadrants captures one of the Four Seasons in the year. These 12 divisions are named after the twelve constellations or Zodiac Signs in the sky. Each one remains behind the Sun all month long, while the Earth's daily rotation places a different Sign on the Eastern Horizon every 2 hours or so. The angle of Earth's source of light creates an amazing array of angles and harmonic resonant energies; They create the 5 primal angles and the 5 previously mentioned Sacred Solids.

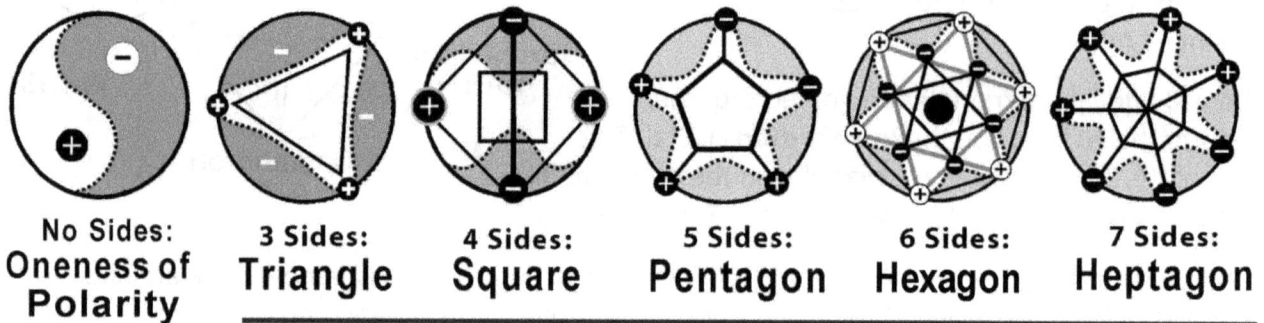

No Sides: Oneness of Polarity	3 Sides: Triangle	4 Sides: Square	5 Sides: Pentagon	6 Sides: Hexagon	7 Sides: Heptagon

The Angles Create Five Geometric Patterns

These images illustrate how the addition of points (into any geometric form) creates a different set of polar and waveform arrangements. This gives us Two-Dimensional versions of what we saw in the Three-Dimensional Sacred Solids. The positive areas in the field are illustrated in the white-lit areas in each triangle. The negative polar areas are captured in the gray portions.

Illustration 1 of the formless **Yin/Yang** symbol, captures the concept of balanced polarity. The addition of another point creates the **3-Sided Triangle**. When another point is added, the **4 corners** of the **Square** take form. Add another, and the **5-Sided Pentagon** appears. Here, one polar charge dominates over the other. All sense of balance is out of the window. This enables the creation of new forms of being.

Next in line is the **6-Sided Hexagon**. This form is actually composed of two triangles. One Hexagon is composed of 6 feminine points. (They are seen in the two black-dotted triangles). The other Hexagon has an overlay of two triangles with "white or masculine-charged points". The *totality* of the *cycle of creation* is captured in these two Hexagons. Each polar combination forms the religious symbol of the *Star of David* and the alternating polarities that we see in the **12 Master Zodiac Divisions** in all astrology charts.

When the last point is added, the odd 51.4 degree angles on the **7-Sided Heptagon** are formed. This weighs the polar force in one direction—far more than what we see in the Pentagon. With both of these uneven pieces, the turn of a few minutes can place these points in a differently polarized sector. That is why astrologers maintain that these two angles often bring unique and surprising alterations into one's life.

This is a little complex, but it shows how the angles create different shapes and forms—and how they structure all physical manifestations.

The Angles of Separation (*Squares and Oppositions*)

Squares and Oppositions create points of stress in the chart. This is because the component on one end is always *aimed in a different direction* than the other. The nature of this separation is defined by the Signs, Houses and aspects of the components. Usually, the point with the strongest planets tells of the direction, in which certain energies will be pulled.

Square Aspects, *Angles A & B, B &C, C&D and D&A:* All squaring points usually consist of Signs of opposite polarity. The transiting component on each point tells **WHAT** activity is in progress. As with all aspects, the **Signs** (and their **House** of placement) tell **WHERE** the activity will occur, and the area in one's life that will be affected by the aspect.

Opposition Aspects, *Lines A&C* and *B&D:* Both points sit on opposite sides of the wheel, and they likely share the same polarity. Being fully separated from each other, they divide the chart in half, as they open the gates to both sides of the wheel. It is time to let go, and take a new course of action. The stress is deciding which way to go, since each of the points are aimed in opposite directions. The placement of dominant planets in one half, will tell you where to place your attention.

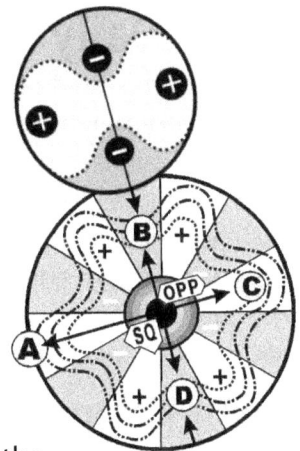

The Angles of Inclusion (Trines, Sextiles, Conjunctions)

The Trine's 120 degree separation usually connects components with the same Mode and Element. The joining of these three resonating and patterning forces completes the trinity. In three dimensions, this triangular arrangement builds the pyramid—the building block of all physical creation!

The Sextile angle of 60 degrees links points that share *the same polarity*. The overlaying of these two triangles (of commonly-charged elements) forms the Six-Pointed Star. The outer points on this star contain the six positive (+) charged points of the Fire and Air elements. On the inset portions of the star, the six feminine (-) points appear. In the chart, they represent the positions of the **12 Masculine and Feminine Zodiac Signs**.

The Conjunction's maximum orb of separation is 8 degrees. Here, components reside on or near the same spot on the wheel. (See D&E). This placement of two or more objects in one area, combines the creative powers of the conjoined units. Together, they impact this singular point in the chart. Therefore, it is considered to be the most powerful aspect.

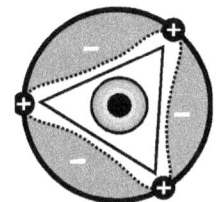

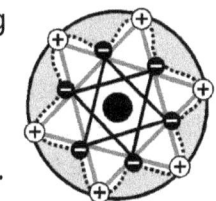

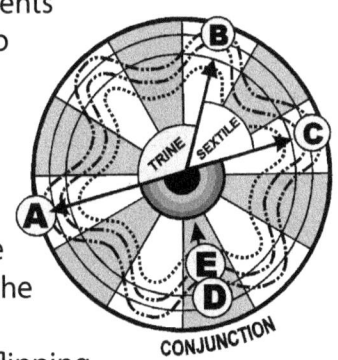

The Angles of Distinction (Quintiles and Septiles)

The Quintile angle breaks the circle into five 72 degree segments. This angle creates the five-sided **Pentagon**. In 3-D, this generates the **dodecahedron**, the entangling soccer ball and **Sacred Solid**—that creates everything in the Universe. As suggested earlier, this form's arrangement of "flipping mirrors" is what merges the masculine and feminine forces into one.

This five-pointed form also represents the form of the human body. At the top, the head connects to the heavens above. To the sides, the arms reach out to handcraft creations, to support our needs. Below, the two legs carry the body to distant places, so that it can gather in the bounty, that will sustain it in the years ahead.

The Septile's 51.42+ degrees of separation forms the seven-sided **Heptagon**.

The MAGIC of this minor aspect is that, like Pi (π), this degree is never fully defined. Some say it is rarely experienced—except during moments of spiritual exhilaration!

This aspect in a chart gives us people who find meaning in their religious or artistic pursuits. With this complex aspect, it is clear that they are many angles (angels?) on the head of every pin. They can not be defined, but it's a joy to imagine what they will do.

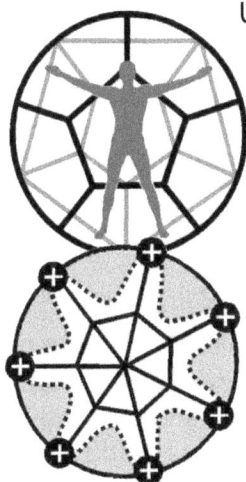

Next, we will look at the impact that these angles have the chart.

The Daily and Yearly Cycles of the Sun:

The ancient stargazers believed they lived in the center of the Universe —and *everything* revolved around their "flat Earth homes". Today, we know the Sun is in the center, and it is our planets 23.5 degree axis tilt, that creates the illusion that the Sun is rising and falling in the sky in its regular daily and seasonal cycles. This makes their charts run upside down and backwards. Still, the results are the same.

This is like watching a spinning bicycle wheel; When you view it from the other side, the wheel spins in the opposite direction, but East remains on the same side.

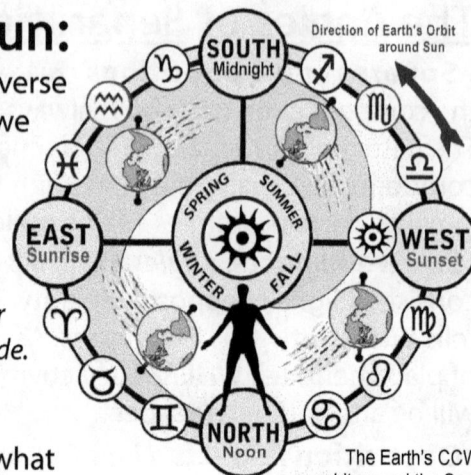

Direction of Earth's Orbit around Sun

The Earth's CCW orbit around the Sun, makes *the Sign behind the Sun* appear to move Clockwise, one Sign every month.

The Compass points are flipped in the Chart

With this "southern orientation", these budding astrologers charted what they saw in the sky. **North** *was placed on the **bottom of their charts** and **East** was on the **left**. In each day's morning light, they saw that the *Sun, Moon* and *stars* would all *rise* in the **East**—and then rotate to the **North** to reach their **peak** at High Noon. In time, they recognized that a different **Rising Sign*** would appear behind the morning Sun in around every 2 hours—and that a new Sign would appear behind the morning Sun in every lunar cycle.

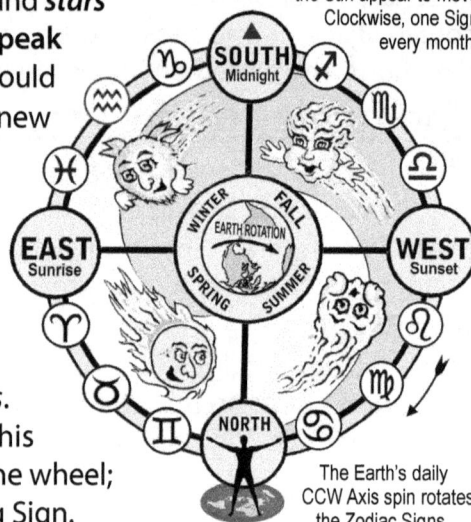

With this flipped chart, the Sun's CCW transit captures the changes in the seasons, as it aligns with another Sign in the wheel. The graphic shows **Aries** rising on the **Spring Equinox. Taurus** gives us mid-spring. When the Sun aligns with **Cancer** and it rises in the Eastern morning light, the Earth's axis is fully tilted to the Sun. Here, at **Noon** on the **Summer Solstice**, the Sun was at **its highest point** *above their homes*. This is why **Cancer**'s **4th House**** is on the bottom of the chart, and this became the format for their charts. These Houses set the spokes in the wheel; They do not move, but the Signs on the Houses are set by one's Rising Sign.

The Earth's daily CCW Axis spin rotates the Zodiac Signs Clockwise, one Sign, every 2 hours.

[*See Rising Signs, page 26 . **See Houses , page 18].

These Cycles Create the Earth's Biorhythmic Patterns

With this, these budding astrologers came to recognize that the different qualities of light in each of these seasons were not only changing the growth of plants and the habits of animals on the planets, they were also affecting the character of their friends and family. The first distinction was seen in those who had a majority of their components above or below the horizontal line in their charts.

The Horizontal Line (The Division between Day & Night)
When Light reigns in the Northern Hemisphere....

When **Aries** peeks over the Eastern horizon, the Earth's axis tilt to the Sun brings the 1st day of dominant light into the Northern hemisphere. Here, the Signs of **Aries** thru **Virgo** appear behind the Sun—to start and complete the seasons of **Spring** and **Summer**. Somehow, these astrologers recognized that the family members who had their Suns—and/or a majority of their components in this half of the chart—often expressed a sunny sense of self, and a "can do" attitude, when they interacted with others. That is why the Houses in this Northern Hemisphere are all ruled by the **Personal Planets**. *(See planets, page 21.)*

When Darkness dominates in the Southern Hemisphere...

If most of your planets are in the "upper dark half" of the chart—you are likely a person, who is less "sun or self-oriented". Save for Venus' rulership of Libra, all of the planets in this half are ruled by the **Transpersonal Planets**. The planets here are usually expressed unconsciously, and this makes these people more private and contemplative—for they derive their energy from their interaction with their own inner world of personal values—rather than outside sources.

The Vertical Line of Division (Recognition of the Waxing & Waning Lights)

The **Meridian** (or vertical line in a chart) connects the Earth's North and South poles, and this creates the East and West sectors in the chart. **The Left** or **Eastern Half** is the time in the day (and in the year), when the Sun begins and completes it building or waxing phase. **The Right** or **Western Half** in the chart is where the light begins its regular daily and seasonal transitions into darkness.

The "Waxing Light" in the Eastern Hemisphere

The Sun's waxing phase begins at the top of the chart, on what astrologers call the **Midheaven**. Here, it is the **Winter Solstice**, where (at Midnight) the **Capricorn** Sun begins its northward climb in the sky. *Everything is looking UP!* In the 2 months after, the Sun aligns with **Aquarius** and **Pisces** to brighten up the Earth. Next, after **Aries**, **Taurus** and **Gemini** take their turns behind the Sun, this half-year of waxing light comes to an end.

When major components are found in the Eastern or left half of the chart, we find individuals who are *highly driven by the building light* and the Cardinal drive of **Capricorn** *and* **Aries**. These folks are self-motivated, strong-willed and determined to increase the "light of their personal Suns". They are the self-starters and leaders, who immediately take action, to make things happen, as they charge undaunted down their personal paths of destiny. Some are highly independent, also intolerant of others who can't agree with their opinions.

The Western Hemisphere's Waning Light

When the Sun crosses the meridian, to plant itself on the chart's Northern point (or **Nadir**) —the dynamics are opposite. For here, the light begins its waning phase on the **Summer Solstice**. **Leo** and **Virgo** follow, to take the Earth into **Libra's Fall Equinox**. Next, with the Sun's passage thru the Signs of **Scorpio** and **Sagittarius**, this half year of waning light comes to an end.

Individual who have a large number of component on this dark side of the circle are guided by the Cardinal Waters of **Cancer** and the balancing force of Libra. They desire to work with others, so they can improve the content in their immediate environment. That is why they work best in partnerships and/or groups.

The Planets in this western hemisphere are "other-oriented". One's personal desires often appear to be in the "hands of destiny". These people need to seize the moment and not bend to the demands of others.

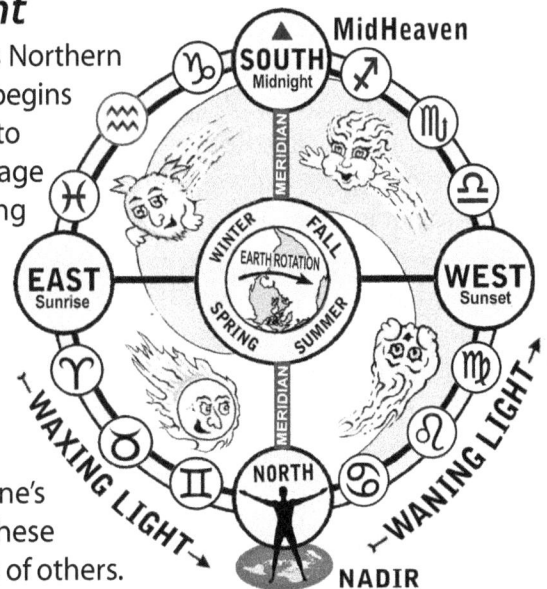

How Earth's Axis Tilt Changes the Seasons

This illustration shows the Earth, as it makes its CCW orbit around the Sun. It also shows how the Sign behind the Sun is always in the opposite Sign of the one—in which the Earth is placed!

In this image, Earth is in the Sign of **Capricorn** and the Sign of **Cancer** is seen **behind the Sun**. Appropriately, at this time, the Earth's North Pole is fully tilted to the Sun, to begin the season of Summer in the northern hemisphere. Meanwhile, on the southern half of the globe, the South Pole is tilted away from the Sun, to start their Winter Solstice.

Unlike Western Astrology, **Vedic Astrologers** interpret the **Sidereal** positions of the stars, as they were thousands of years ago. This long range view supports the concept of karma, where every action has its' own corresponding reaction. Meanwhile, **Tropical Astrologers** base their work on the Earth's position to the Sun and the modal and elemental patterns of the season. That is what is used in this book.

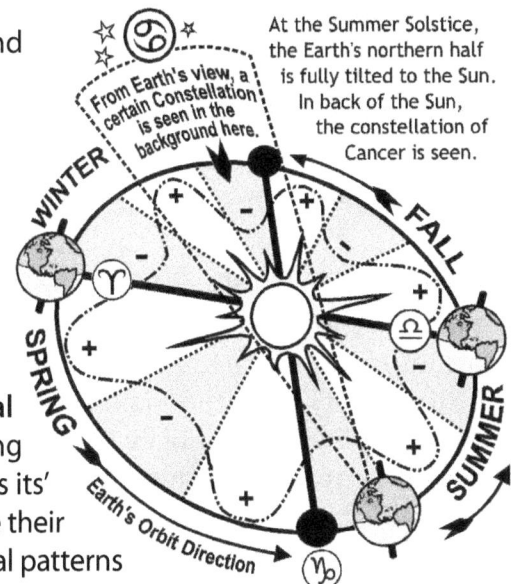

Next, the Modal patterns and Elemental forces are examined. 9

~ The Four Elements ~

Wondrously placed at the right place in space, our planet's year-long orbit brings an array of varying temperatures. The moments, with extra light and heat, turn a solid form into liquid; A bit more heat transforms a liquid into a gas. Add a few more degrees and a solid bursts into flame! These four states gave astrologers a method to classify Nature's many manifestations into four comparative categories of "vibrational force"—those exhibited in the **Four Elements: Fire, Earth, Air** and **Water**.

All things in each group, share a commonality with the others—be it their physical state, vibratory nature or commonness in subject matter, endeavor, thought, principle or manner of expression. Everything that shares a synchronous or sympathetic connection—is placed in one of these four elemental categories.

This classification method includes all forms of live and inanimate objects (natural or human made). For example, the Fixed Earth of *Taurus* is associated with land and banking; *Libra's* equinoctial qualities empower thoughts that create balance and fairness—those professed in the field of law. The subjects and rulerships for each of the Signs are discussed in the Sun Sign sections, that begin on page 35.

The Masculine Elements: Fire & Air

At the six positive points in the wheel, the light waves are at their peak—to generative the expansive actions, gestures and thoughts, that reside in the elements of **Fire** and **Air**.

In the Element of **Fire**, the creative force is in its purest state. This abundance of light and heat ignites mannerisms of great intensity and combustibility. Here, the intangible essence of Desire, Will and Inspiration manifests in the *Spark of Spirit*—that we see in the three Fire Signs: **Aries**, **Leo** and **Sagittarius.**

Like Fire, the vibrational forces in the Element of **Air** are also expansive and positively charged—but far less intense, since the energy is dispersed into greater areas of *mental occupation*. These dynamics emulate qualities suggestive of floating clouds, swirling breezes and funnels of wind. These currents stir the minds of astrology's Mental Signs: **Gemini, Libra** and **Aquarius**. These airy qualities resonate with those of Fire.

Fiery **Aries** starts the numbering of the sectors or Houses in the astrology wheel. The triangle of Fire occupies Houses 1, 5 and 9. Air Signs fill the triangle of Houses 3, 7 and 11.* This star-shaped configuration of trine and sextile angles implies that there is compatibility here. Indeed, there is. Fire needs Air to burn, and it is the heat of Fire that allows Air to expand its range of occupation. *[See Houses on page 21].*

The Feminine Elements: Earth & Water

The six positively-charged points in the wheel are each followed by a point of feminine polarity. As the gray areas show, these internalizing (+charged) forces are countering the expansive Fire and Air Elements. It brings the consolidated states, that we find in the Elements: **Earth** and **Water**.

Earth defines the substance of "physical matter".

With Nature's assemblage, configuration and application of earthy materials, the senses are aroused in the Earth Signs: **Taurus, Virgo** and **Capricorn**.

Water is the Element of transformation. Increase the heat (*Fire*) and the water turns into steam (*Air*); Cool the clouds of *steam* and they liquefy into *rain*. Cool the rain a few more degrees, and the water turns into the solidity of *ice*. The liquid feelers of **Cancer, Scorpio** and **Pisces** coat, permeate and meld everything they touch. The compatibility of these two feminine Elements is apparent. Earth contains Water, while Water loosens Earth—to bring it to life, in the chart's Houses 2, 6 and 10. The Universal Solvent of Water melds the physical forms together, in Houses 4, 8 and 12.

When the feminine and masculine forces interact with each other, the Universe is filled with a giant array of physical forms. When these formations are pushed, squeezed and twisted by the **Three Modal Actions** —the possibilities are endless!

How the Modes work

As mentioned in the forward, this author contents that it is we suggested that all of the formations on our planet are created by the Earth's daily and yearly CCW spin—and the macro and micro angles of the Sun to Earth's equinoctial plane and its magnetic and polar fields. This constant repetition of angles and degrees (on both sides of the wheel) creates the patterns of the three modes. They work something like this:

Every circular event *starts with a directed movement*—be it the aiming of a beam of light or a rock whirling thru space. When the Sun's crosses of the Earth's compass points, the Sun's light is aimed in a new **Cardinal** direction, to start a new phase of creation.

With any diversion from this path, there is a need to define a new *Fixed center* and the radius of a new circle or cycle of activity. With this definition of fixed

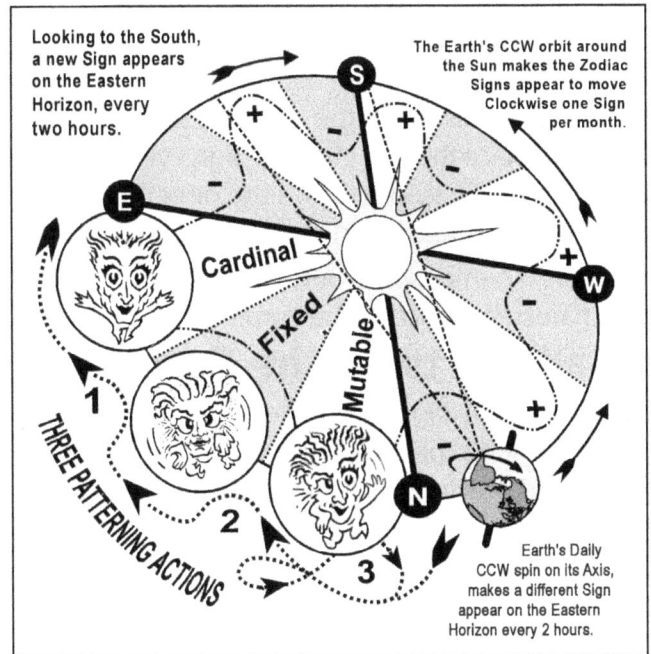

Looking to the South, a new Sign appears on the Eastern Horizon, every two hours.

The Earth's CCW orbit around the Sun makes the Zodiac Signs appear to move Clockwise one Sign per month.

THREE PATTERNING ACTIONS

Cardinal
Fixed
Mutable

Earth's Daily CCW spin on its Axis, makes a different Sign appear on the Eastern Horizon every 2 hours.

space, *Mutable adjustments* are needed—to weave and blend the ends together and make the changes that will allow another round of modal actions to begin. Astrologers call these three patterns of action the **Cardinal, Fixed and Mutable Modes!** They imply what their names suggest, and they show how each mode counters the action of the previous. In the chart, each mode represents one of the three months in a season. Each Season fills one of the four quadrants in a chart.

The 3 Patterning Modes Create the 4 Seasons in a Year

For many years, the ancients observed the repetitive orbits of the Sun and Moon. Perhaps it was with the lunar tides, where they first saw these three repeating patterns—as the changing positions of the Moon brought a surging tide, a period of resting water and then its return to its place of origin. In time, these astute observers realized that each of these three operating Modes were bringing a switch in polarity, and a countering action to the previous mode. They believed these activities were forming the physical arrangements in all things above and below. This became the foundation of all future science.

These three modal patterns are activated in each of the four seasons. At each of the seasonal starting points (**Step1**), the Sun begins it movement into a new **Cardinal** direction. With the Sun's entrance into middle of the season (**Step 2**), the **Mode of Fixity** is activated, as the polar shift places all things on hold.

The final polar shift brings **Step 3: The Mutable Modes**. They make the adjustments and chances that are needed, to bring the season to an end.

In 4 seasons, these 3 steps are repeated, to give the year its 12 combinations of Modes and Elements. Each of these define the qualities of one of the 12 Zodiac Signs.

For simplicity's sale, the illustration only shows the season of Spring, i.e., the first quadrant in the Cross. It shows how the force of Cardinality starts each of the seasons, when a Cardinal Sign appears on the Eastern Horizon—and how one month later, *the Fixed Force arrives in the East,* to manifest the new formations in the season. In the final month of the season, these holding patterns are divided, to mix the two previous actions into the new arrangements, that will prepare the Earth for the new season ahead.

Precession of the Equinoxes:

*With the gradual rotation of Earth's poles, the North Pole rotates **backwards** one Sign—in about every 2,000 years. This changes the Sign on the Eastern horizon.*

That is why, today—the constellation of Aquarius (rather than that of Aries) is behind the Sun, on the Spring Equinox.

Aries rose on the eastern horizon around 4,000 years ago. At the time of Christ, **Pisces** was there. Today, with the internet, we are in the **Age of Aquarius!** This precession idea is used in "sidereal astrology". However, this book uses the original version with **Aries** ruling the 1st House—and it works! It supports the idea that it is the angle of Earth's Equator to the Sun, that makes all of this happen.

The Cardinal Points
Everything has to start —to go somewhere.

Once again, to match the astrology chart, North is placed on the bottom and this sends the Sun and Signs rotating CCW in the wheel, to place the Sun in a new Sign every month. Meanwhile, the Earth's daily spin reverses the direction, to plant the Sun and a different Rising Sign in the East, every two hours.

Here, we'll demonstrate how these Cardinal Forces define the character of each of the Cardinal Zodiac Signs.

The order of the Signs, and the Sun's yearly cycle run Clockwise in the chart.

In its' Daily cycle, the Sun moves CCW to place a new Sign on the Eastern Horizon in every two hours.

It all starts on the Cardinal Cross

When the Sun aligns with one of the four Cardinal compass points, it marks the starting point of one of the four seasons. As defined previously, **the horizontal line** is where the masculine Signs of **Aries** and **Libra** define the months of the two Equinoxes, where the Earth's two hemispheres experience an equal balance of light.

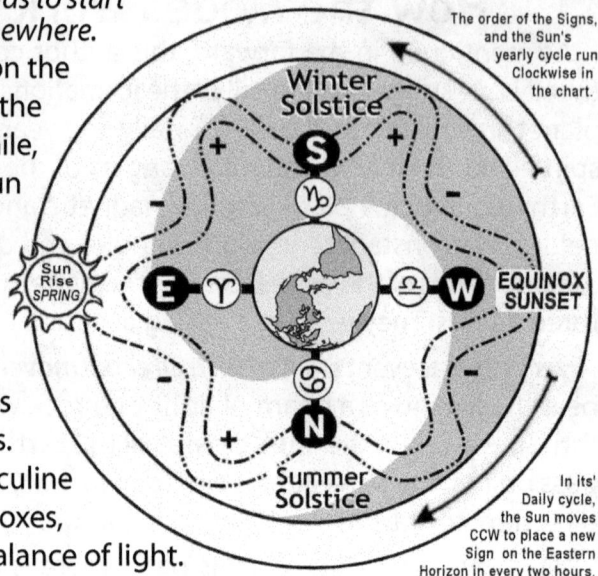

On the vertical meridian, the receptive Signs of **Cancer** and **Capricorn** appear at the **Solstices**. These points define the starting points of the waxing and waning phases in the Sun's light. On the left side of the wheel, the light is building. On the right, the Sun begins its journey into night.

What to expect, when the Cardinal Signs appear:

All Cardinal components in one's chart instill a desire to "create movement"—in the House or area where they're located. Also, when a component crosses or transits one of the Grand Cross points in your chart, you can expect a noticeable redirection in that area of your life. The nature of this action is determined by the Signs on the cross points in the chart. These actions become "the cross you bear" in your life.

On the horizontal line, the masculine Fire of **Aries** and the Air of **Libra** respectively surge in a forward and sideways direction! In the feminine or receptive Signs of **Cancer** and **Capricorn**, the watery and earthy forces are internalized, and then directed in a downward or upward direction.

The Masculine Cardinal Signs
The Forward Charge of Fire: Aries

When the Sun enters the Sign of *Aries*, the Sun is on the equator, to light both portions of the Earth with an equal amount of light. Notably, in the northern hemisphere, the light begins its domination over the night, for the first time in this yearly cycle. This ignites the **Cardinal Fire**—to begin another creative adventure, and the season of Spring.

This incredible rush of light accelerates the creative urges, to drive all souls to project and fulfill the self expressions of their own personal solar light. Those with strong Aries components often display the highly directed force of Cardinal Fire, as they charge head-first down the path. This back-to-front movement gives the Ram its swept-back eyebrows and its convex and vertically stretched face.

The Side-to-Side Spread of Air: Libra

Six months later, it is the **Fall Equinox** in the northern hemisphere*. Here, as the Sun drops below the equator, the Sign of **Libra** gently eases this half of the globe into the darker half of the year. Here, the forward drive of the Ram is redirected, as the forces of **Cardinal Air** sweep the energy off to the sides in a horizontal direction. This redirection inspires individuals to interact with others, and the surroundings—outside their personal worlds!

Hereon, all seasonal references apply to the northern hemisphere; It is the opposite season in the Southern Hemisphere.

This horizontal spread of energy, shapes the physical traits of Libra. Below the level eyebrows, the widespread almond eyes radiate sparkles of light, as they dart from side to side. The mouth stretches the cheeks wide to the sides, to form the V-shaped cherubic Libra smile.

The Feminine Cardinal Signs
Water Flows Down to the Sea: Cancer

At the **Summer Solstice**, the Sun is at its highest point in the sky. Here, the Sun begins its six-month downward journey into Winter's night. This waning light (and the polar switch from positive to negative) brings an emotional need—to restrain the expansive impulses of the Aries' season, and look inward—to find a place of comfort in a turbulent world.

With the feminine water of **Cancer**, there is a need to secure a base and a home, to store the nurturing substances, that will be needed, to support the family of the Cancer Crab. This downward draw of **Cardinal Water** pulls Cancer's eyes and wavy brows low on the face, as it anchors them between the ballooning temples. The high forehead, round temples and receded chin mock the shape of the shell of a crab.

The Upward Climb of Earth: Capricorn

At the **Winter Solstice**, the Sun is at its lowest point below the horizon. Here, the year starts anew, as the Sun begins its upward climb in the sky. *It's all up from here!* That's why Capricorns are always looking up, as they climb to seek a higher position in life.

This force of **Cardinal Earth** supports Cancer's protective urges, as it attempts to secure the strategic outer positions—that will help the family to survive, in the many years ahead.

These upward climbing forces shape the goat's physical traits. The mountain's base is formed by the wide cavernous cheek bones. From there, the bony brow and wide-set eyes rise upward and narrow, to form the jagged peak on the upper skull.

Observing Cardinal Expressions in the Personality:

Watch the mannerisms of the Cardinal Signs, and you may immediately see how the pattern of their expressions are different than what we see in the Fixed and Mutable signs. Cardinal actions are well-aimed and also highly directed. This direction is easy to detect; Just watch their body language, as the move about in the world.

Aries and Libra

If you notice a forceful outward drive in their movements, it's likely you are observing one of the masculine **Cardinal Signs: Aries** or **Libra.** If the movement is a "forward thrust of the head" and the person is consistently *in-your face*, it's likely you have encountered an Aries Ram. **Hugh Hefner** (4/09), **Lady GaGa** (3/28) and **Leonard Nimoy** (3/26) demonstrate Aries' unstoppable force.

If this consuming presence surrounds you with a force that seems to disarm, rather than exasperate tensions, it is likely you are in contact with a Libra. Watch for that unmistakable smile and the horizontally stretched lines in the face. These features are seen in **Jimmy Carter** (10/01), **Sigourney Weaver** (10/8) and **Gwyneth Paltrow** (9/28).

Cancer and Capricorn

If a *"pulling force"* is attracting your attention, it is likely that your are being drawn in by the femininely-charged fields of the **Cardinal Water** and **Earth** Signs of **Cancer** or **Capricorn.**

If you see the depth of the ocean in their eyes, and the beaming lunar face offers you a bowl of yummy soup—you're being mothered by a Cancer Crab! **Meryl Streep** (5/22), **Harrison Ford** (7/13) and **Linda Ronstadt** (7/15) display the liquid qualities of Cancer's surging tides.

If the pull is void of emotions (and very persistent), you are likely being accosted by a goat. Tenaciously, they will continue to "pull your strings". This upward push can be seen in the faces of **Dave Matthews** (1/9), **Denzel Washington** (12/28) and **Mary Tyler Moore** (12/29).

The Fixed Mid-Points
Go Ahead, Make My Day!

Every month, the Sun moves clockwise 30 degrees. When it enters the middle month of each season, the forces are "caught in the center"—to manifest the fixed physical, spiritual, emotional and mental formations of the four Fixed Signs: **Taurus, Leo, Scorpio** and **Aquarius**. This containment creates the holding pattern, that shapes the square and rectangular features of fixity.

In the feminine Signs of **Taurus** and **Scorpio**, these internally fixed wire-frames respectively—create all physical matter, and all forms of life.

With the Masculine Signs, this fixed force is externalized, to create the magnetic and radiating forces of **Leo** and **Aquarius**. It is the glow of *Leo's Fixed Fire* that attracts the attention of others, and then inspires them to contribute to the Lion's creative endeavors.

Leo's vision is defined, when the *Fixed Air of Aquarius* transmits the thoughts and ideas out to of others. This melding of ideas into a common consensus, makes future changes possible.

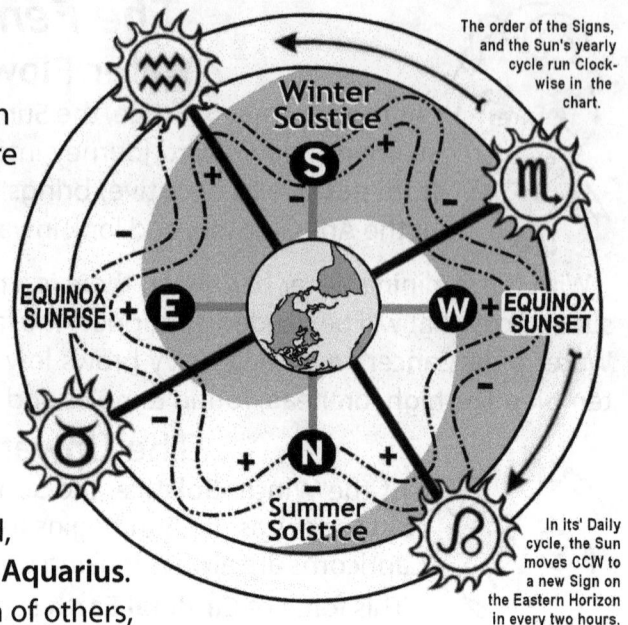

The order of the Signs, and the Sun's yearly cycle run Clockwise in the chart.

In its' Daily cycle, the Sun moves CCW to a new Sign on the Eastern Horizon in every two hours.

The Feminine Fixed Signs
The Definition of Physical Form: Taurus

In the middle of the Spring season, the roots sink deeply into the Earth—to clutch onto the earthy substances, that will become the building blocks of all physical creations. With **Aries**, we saw the light. Now, in this month of the greatest physical growth, we can use our Taurus senses of touch, taste and hearing, to define the material worth of what Nature has given us in our surroundings.

In moments of contented grazing, the Taurus Bull's senses are highly aroused. Watch how the eyebrows fold down in the middle, as the large bovine eyes focus on substances of beauty. There, you'll see this creature's sly smile of contentment, as he or she gathers in the aromas from a flower, or hears the music of buzzing bees. It is these Taurus senses, that make life so delightful.

The Containment of Emotions: Scorpio

At the opposite end of the month of Taurus, it is the middle of the Fall season. Here, the forces are stilled by the encroaching darkness of the Scorpio Sun. Resources are becoming harder to find, and our feelings tell us that we need to evaluate "all of the useless stuff", that we have accumulated, since last Spring.

It is time to decide what is important, and what has real value and worth! With the help of the fixed and unwavering emotions of Scorpio, we will know what to hold on to—and what to eliminate!

In Scorpio's fixed waters, there is an urge to create a bridge—to connect the feminine and masculine forces. This linking of these opposing polarities gives individuals the ability to connect to their own internal source of power—the one that rejuvenates and keeps the body healthy! It also insures the continuance of life.

When an individual emotionally connects with—and shares resources with others—the power of all of the participants increases exponentially. With this empowerment, this convocation of Eagles is ready to fly away—and soar to unimaginable heights.

14

The Masculine Fixed Signs
Containment of Fire and Spiritual Desires: LEO

In the doldrums of Mid-Summer, the rays of the fiery Sun are intensely focused, to spotlight Summer's "last hurrah". Here, the concentration of warmth creates a luminous glow and an environment, that is bright and colorful. With all of this, the Leo Lion is inspired to make "the show" even more spectacular!

When Leo's grandiose visions are playfully presented to others, they quickly draw attention. This feedback fuels Leo's inner fires—and it often sparks a spectacular array of creative visions. They'll be so inspiring, that everyone will want to contribute to the show.

The Connecting of Collective Thoughts: Aquarius

In the midst of Winter's darkness, the building light of Capricorn is fully recognized, as the Fixed Air of Aquarius confirms to all—*brighter days are lying ahead*! This idea instills an unwavering sense of optimism and a self-sustaining sense of hope.

Being on the opposite side of Leo, Aquarius sees everything thru the eyes of others. This enables these Fixed Air souls to tune into—and then reshape the thoughts of others! This water-bearer's flood of insights often formats an array of new opinions and new ways of thinking—in large groups of people!

Observing Fixed Expressions in the Personality:

Fixed expressions show *a holding of center* and a boxing of energies—inside and outside the self. That is why most of America's earlier network news teams were made up of Fixed Sign people. We like our *Anchors* to be emotionally unflappable and of course, capable of pouring out a steady uninterrupted flow of words. Here, fixed newscasters make up this entire photo collection.

Taurus and Scorpio

If you see a "holding pattern" and a deeply internalized focus of energy, it's likely you are observing one of the **Feminine Fixed Signs**.

If the person appears stubborn and resistant to movement, you're likely grazing with a contented cow or bull. (The bovine eyes are a give-away). **Brian Williams** (5/05), **Mike Wallace** (5/09) and the legendary **Edward R. Murrow** (4/25) are heavyweight Taurus anchors.

If you feel the presence of submerged emotions and you can't escape the draw of those hypnotic eyes, then you are being drawn into the mysterious world of a Scorpio. Anchors **Walter Cronkite** (11/04), **Dan Rather** (10/31) and **Jane Pauley** (10/31) showed us Scorpio's incredible emotional control, even in the most trying of events.

Leo and Aquarius

It's hard to visualize an action that is *holding* and *reaching out* at the same time, but this is the case with the **Masculine Fixed Signs**—Leo and Aquarius. They have a gift for attracting the attention of others, so they can connect to and communicate their ideas OUT to others.

If you give someone a compliment—and they take on a fixed and radiant glow—then you're likely in the presence of a Leo. This aura of fixed confidence was proudly presented by **Peter Jennings** (7/29), **Linda Ellerbee** (8/15) and **Connie Chung**. (8/20).

Give an Aquarius a compliment and it'll likely go unnoticed. Give them an idea and their eyes will sparkle with electricity, as their minds connect to a surprising array of thoughts. **Tom Brokaw** (2/06), **Ted Koppel** (2/08) and **Jessica Savitch** (2/01) show us this gift of fixed air.

15

The Mutable Points

Now that we've got it made,
it is time to make some changes.

With another 30 degree turn of the cross, we find the points, where the Sun is entering the final month in each of the four seasons.

It is time to make the internal and external adjustments to the previous Cardinal and Fixed actions. With this, we can bring the previous lessons to completion and make the preparations, we will need in the new season ahead.

Caught between the *Stop* and the *Go* (the Fixed and the Cardinal), these Mutable energies run in a Mobius pattern, stirring up things inside and out. These mixing forces are seen in the twisted and skewed features of the four **Mutable Signs: Gemini**, **Virgo**, **Sagittarius** and **Pisces**.

The order of the Signs and the Sun's yearly cycle run Clockwise in the chart.

In its' Daily cycle, the Sun moves CW to place a new Sign on the Eastern Horizon in every two hours.

Mutable energy examines all of the angles, from all sides—as it decides "which way to go". With these mixing actions, preparations are being made to start another Cardinal pattern, that will bring the Earth another month, season—and/or another new year of creation!

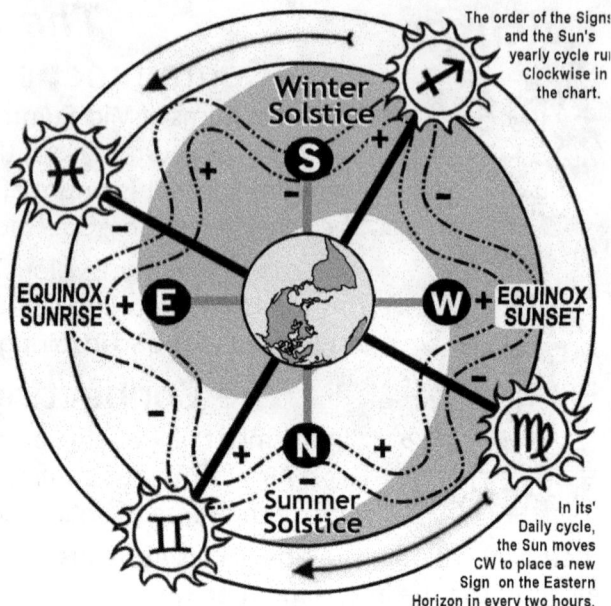

The Feminine Mutable Signs

When something needs to be changed, some of us find it best to start by breaking things into their smaller pieces, so we can analyze how they be rearranged into a more complex and greater whole. Those with this view, often have their Suns in the **Feminine Mutable Signs** of **Virgo** and **Pisces**.

Creating Perfection in the Physical World: Virgo

Summer's end brings an abundant harvest of earthy delights. Here, with the **Mutable Earth** of **Virgo**, there is an urge to breakdown, analyze, sort, clean and preserve these offerings—so that they can sustain us, in the winter months ahead.

With **Virgo**, this understanding of the "workable pieces" brings the knowledge, that will serve the needs and health of others. The task of bringing them together—to form more workable wholes—is the job of the **Mutable Water Sign** of **Pisces**.

The Unification of Emotional Arrangements: Pisces

At **Winter**'s end, multilevel changes begin, as the melting waters of **Pisces** flow freely, once again. Here, all of the previous actions, physical formations, intents and feelings are stirred together in the universal solvent of water. This merging of multiple arrangements (into larger wholes) plants the seeds, that will enable all to believe that every dream is possible!

When the eyes of the Pisces fish peer off in two directions—everything is felt and seen on both sides. This makes it difficult to determine the course that lies ahead. Fortunately, Pisces' instinctual feelings are telling them that their path of destiny will soon be revealed—and it will appear in the Spring, when the Sun enters **Aries**.

The Masculine Mutable Signs

With the Feminine Mutable Signs, the internal workings of individual arrangements were analyzed, physically disassembled and transformed. In contrast, when the **Masculine Mutable Signs** appear, it is time to reach out and collect the collective lessons and acquired knowledge of others—and bring them into "the mix". With this, individual creations can grow exponentially—to serve the needs of all of the life on the Earth.

16

The Shifting Winds of the Mind: Gemini

At the end of **Spring**, it is time to prepare the Earth for the upcoming **Summer** season. Last month, **Aries** kick-started the season, as the flowers in **Taurus** emerged from the "seeds of **Pisces**". Now in full bloom, the swirling winds of **Gemini** are cross-pollinating Nature's future seeds, to bring new varieties of fruit to the world.

Mutable Air activates the dueling personalities of the Gemini twins. With the infusion of this Sign's ruling planet Mercury, most Geminis appear to have two interacting faces. This gives them rapid blinking eyes and hand movements, that run in opposite directions.

The Unbound Fire of Exalted Desires: Sagittarius

In the last month of the **Fall Season**, the Earth approaches the darkest day of the year. Fortunately, our acquired knowledge tells us that the Sun will soon rise again—to bring a new round of building light—and another year of unlimited possibilities!

It is **Mutable Fire** that brings a positive change in attitude—for it sparks one's desire to free one's self from all restraints. With this, grander creative actions can be pursued, as these unbridled **Centaurs** gallop freely into the New Year ahead. It will be the spirit of *Sagittarius*—and the fiery arrows of the *Archer*—that will light the path ahead—and inspire all of humanity to pursue their greatest desires. Why not? All things are possible!

Observing Mutable Expressions in Others:

So far, we have detected the directed force of **Cardinality** and the on-hold expressions of **Fixity**. If neither of these exist—and the modal nature is indefinable and constantly changing—then you can suspect the presence of a **Mutable Sign**.

Gemini and Sagittarius

If you sense an expansive twisting energy, spinning all around you—it's likely you encountered a masculine Mutable Sign. If you see electrical sparks, and you hear a didactic stream of chatter, then you're likely having a conversation with a Gemini. **Natalie Portman** (6/9), **Clint Eastwood** (6/31) and **Angelina Jolie** (7/04) are all masters of this verbal spin.

If you being interrupted in the middle of every sentence, and the subject matter constantly takes quantum leaps in its content, then you caught the momentary attention span of a **Sagittarius**. These fiery ponies, like **Ben Stiller** (11/30), **Christina Aguilera** (12/18), and **Brad Pitt** (12/18) will always brighten your day.

Virgo and Pisces

The Feminine Mutable Signs seem to draw us into the twisting vortex of "Alice's Rabbit Hole", where surroundings subtly morph and change—to alter the nature of the hole, and "the whole".

If the person is noticeably critical of the imperfections in their surroundings, and they steadily offer their services to make them better—you're likely in the presence of a **Virgo**.

Cameron Diaz (8/30), **Sean Connery** (8/25) and **Beyonce** (9/01) are perfect examples of **Virgo**'s meticulous nature, but if the only reaction is a dreamy look of detachment, then you are caught in a webbed net with a **Pisces** fish. The imaginations of **Bon Jovi** (3/2), **Joanne Woodward** (2/27) and **Michael Caine** (3/14) has helped us to escape from the trappings of a mundane world.

The Twelve Houses in the chart

The 12 divisions (i.e., Houses) in the chart run in the order of the Signs, as they appear in the skies above. **The Houses do not move**, but the Signs on the cusps of all of the Houses can be altered by the Rising Sign in the East. To explain all of this, let's imagine that **the chart** is a **computer program** on its own **master hard drive**:

Within this software, the chart defines the connections that may occur between any Houses, Signs or Planets in the chart. For example, **House #1** contains the core data for **Aries**. It instructions all components in this House to *Assert and activate one's personal identity*. All the while, **House #2**'s provides data on how to *deal with the values and possessions of* **Taurus**. This idea continues thru all Signs and Houses.

….. and there's the effects of the Rising Sign:

When one's time-of-birth places a different Rising Sign on the chart's eastern point, all of the House cusps are altered. The planet that rules your 1st House is highly important, for it represents how you connected to, and create your personal identity. The planetary ruler of the Sign on each of the House cusps also has its own unique impact. For instance, those with *Leo on their 4th House often make their homes a virtual palace, with royal decor everywhere*. Those with *Aquarius on the Midheaven* are often inventors or rebel rousers who communicate their revolutionary ideas for social change, to a larger segment of society.

Another variegating factor is the placement of components in the Houses. They tend to alter the force of the native Sign of each House, and the operating Sign on the cusp.

Descriptions of the Quadrants and then 12 Houses in the Chart

The 1st Quadrant records the activities in the Season of **Spring**. In this initial dominance of solar light, the *Light of Self* is explored. This quadrant consists of the following three steps of self-discovery:

House 1, natural Home of **Aries**. The Rising Sign, Ego, Exploration of Self, The Image projected out to others.

House 2, natural Home of **Taurus**: Personal Values, Possessions and Definition of Self Worth.

House 3, natural Home of **Gemini**: Development of mental and communication skills, thru learning.

The 2nd Quadrant suggests the nature of **Summer's** Solstice and the polar shift at high noon, when the Sun begins its journey into night. The waning light impels us to define our *Sense of Place* and how we interact with the following areas in our surroundings:

House 4, natural Home of **Cancer**: Emotional Base, Security in one's personal home, Motherhood and the nuturing of one's family.

House 5, Home of **Leo**: Creative Will, Children, Theatre, Envisioning of ways to enhance our surroundings.

House 6, Home of **Virgo**: Purification of body and mind by contributing to the improvement of the nearby environment, and serving others.

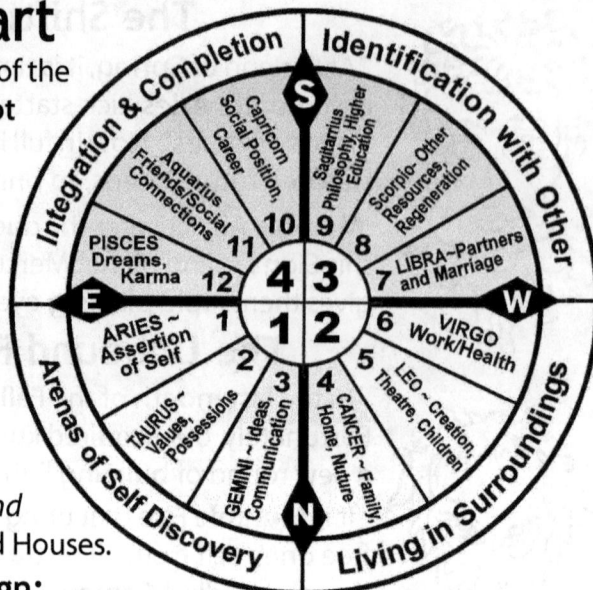

In the 3rd Quadrant, the **Autumn** Sun is in the darker half of the cycle. In this quadrant, one begins the task of Relating to the *Non-Personal realities in the "other world, outside the self"*.

House 7, Home of **Libra**: Enhancement of Mind thru Art, Law, Justice, Partners, Marriage.

House 8, Home of **Scorpio**: Sex, Regeneration, Death, Definition of worth of others. Holding of Resources and the discarding of waste.

House 9, Home of **Sagittarius**: Expansion of Spirituality, higher education and philosophy.

In the Final Quadrant of **Winter**, the light begins to build again. Here, there is a need to *Integrate all of the previous Personal and Non-Personal activities* and bring them into completion.

House 10, home of **Capricorn**: Career, Social Position, Goals and Ambitions, mastering age.

House 11, home of **Aquarius**: Friends, Social Affairs, Collective Consciousness, Inventions.

House 12, Pisces: Karma, Faith and Completion What you sow is what you will receive. It is time to let go, and let a new beginning begin.

Next, we look at how each House works in the wheel.

First Quadrant: Discovery of Self (Recognition of Being)

The 1st Quadrant represents the season of **Spring**, when the Sun crosses over the equator, to bring the "first day of dominate light" into the world. With this awakening, there is as need to recognize and discover one's sense of individuality. This is done when one hones his/her senses, to gather in the knowledge that they communicate to others. These three Signs represent the period in one's life (from birth to pre-teens).

HOUSE #1: ARIES ~ Here I Am!

The **1st House** in this quadrant is the natural home of **Aries**. Here, in the awakening light, **Cardinal Fire** drives all individuals to pursue their personal journey of self-discovery. Transiting planets in this 1st House change one's sense and image of self. Planets placed here at birth, often dictate the physical appearance of one's Rising Sign and the persona that others see on first glance.

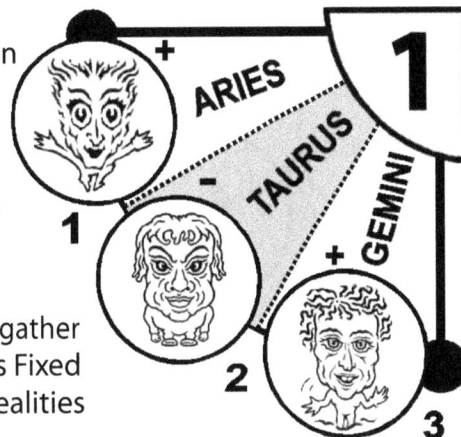

HOUSE #2: TAURUS ~ Definition of Self Worth

With the polar shift to feminine **Taurus**, the senses are activated, to gather in the material needs—that will support one's physical body. In this Fixed Earth House, all enclosed components identify with the physical realities associated with Banking, Farming, Property and Real Estate!

Any planet placed within, or transiting this House (in a manner typical of the planet) affects the way a person views "his/her value and worth" and what actions he/she will take, to protect one's possessions.

HOUSE #3: GEMINI ~ Learning to Think

With Taurus' sensual input, there is an incredible amount of "stuff" to analyze. This House's association with masculine polarity and mutable Air of **Gemini** impels individuals are to reach out and gather in volumes of data, so that they can understand and interact with their surroundings. Components in this House will define how one communicates his/her ideas to siblings, and also passes them on to others. This enhanced curiosity, inspires one to by take short journeys, by using personal forms of transportation.

With these lessons complete, we move into the Second Quadrant, where we find that Houses that bring the lessons, that will able us to relate to, and interact with our surroundings.

Second Quadrant: Living in Surroundings

At the **Summer Solstice**, the year begins its long journey into night. With this reorientation in direction—the polar shift propels individuals to gather in the needed supplies, to sustain their families. To this end, one needs to share his/her visions with neighbors, and then perform the work that will serve others. This is the period of adolescence, where we find our place in our surroundings, and learn to relate to others.

HOUSE #4: CANCER ~ The Base of Comfort

Cardinal Water draws us into the **4th House** (the base of the chart). Here, we find the components that define how we nourish and relate to the family, and the place that we call home.

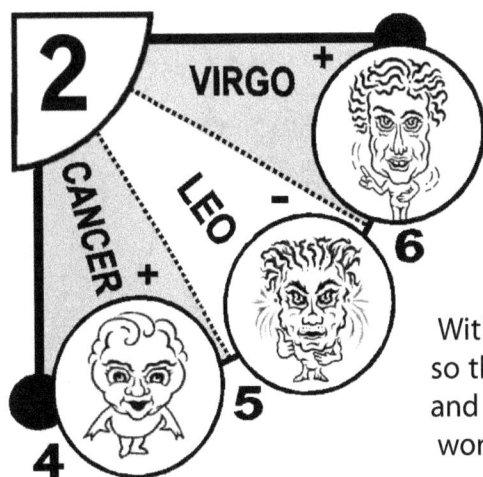

HOUSE #5: LEO ~ Visions of Grander Conditions

In the glowing light of Midsummer, it's time to venture out beyond the comforts of the home—and check out the neighborhood! There, our Leo friends present their visions, on how to improve the community center, or build a playground for children. With their flair, these Lions inspire others to join in, and support the cause.

HOUSE #6: VIRGO ~ Make It Happen & Make It Work!

At Summer's end, it's time to prepare for the chilly nights that lie ahead. With this, individuals need to work with others and perfect their skills, so they can complete the essential tasks, that will serve their families and neighbors! Components in the **6th House** define the nature of one's work and the manner in which a person presents this service to others.

The lessons for "relating to others" begin in the next quadrant.

Third Quadrant: Relating to Others

In Quadrant 3, the Sun is entering the upper half of the chart—and the other half of the year! Here, at the **Fall Equinox**, the *Light of the Sun and the Self* dims, as darkness dominates the upper sky. Components here often suggest how a person reacts to, and values the opinions of others. This is the teen years in one's life, when the act of "relating and interacting with others" becomes the foremost consideration in one's life.

HOUSE #7: LIBRA ~ Marriage and Partnerships

On the other side of the First House of **Aries**, the perspective changes, as the mind learns to see "through the eyes of others". Here, the **Cardinal Air** of Libra desires to find close relationships and partners in life. With love of others, diplomacy and the establishment of fair laws—tensions are disarmed.

HOUSE #8: SCORPIO ~ Other Resources

With **Fall**, things appear lovely, but the darker days and colder nights are telling us that our resources are becoming scarcer. This brings an emotional response, that questions the *real* worth of our **Taurus** possessions, and the value of what we are receiving from others.

In **Scorpio's Fixed Water**, the light barely fills the shadows, but the dim light in the **8th House** is enough—to reveal the mysterious secrets of sex, birth, death and rejuvenation.

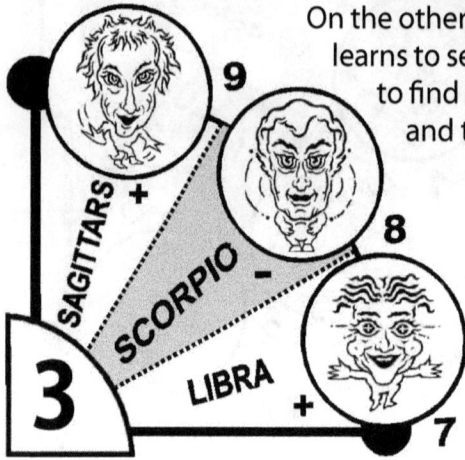

HOUSE #9: SAGITTARIUS ~ Expansion of Mind and Spirit

With this emotional empowerment, individuals are unchained from feelings of doubt. With this, grander visions fill the mind—as the concepts in **Gemini** are expanded by the **Mutable Fire** of **Sagittarius**. In this **9th House**, higher education and the study of philosophical subjects (moral ideals, conscience, justice and the spiritual concepts of divinity) come to light. Long distant travel, foreign languages and all of the subjects that inspire a wider range of consciousness are also associated with this House.

Fourth Quadrant: Integration, Completion & Emotional Union

At the **Winter Solstice,** the Sun is at its lowest point in the sky. However, there is a ray of hope, for we know that the light is building again—and a New Year has begun! This quadrant marks the adult period in our lives, where we learn the important lessons that come with age.

HOUSE #10: CAPRICORN ~ Aspirations and Attainment

As adults, it is time to secure strategic positions in the larger world, beyond our **4th House** homes. After all, no family is secure, when communities and nations fail. This is the lesson in **Capricorn's 10th House**.

Here, we USE the inspired lessons of our Centaur teachers—and the wisdom from distant and ancient cultures. This enriches our knowledge and sense of purpose. With the directed discipline of **Cardinal Earth**, all individuals can hone their professional skills, and build the institutions that will support future goals.

HOUSE #11: AQUARIUS ~ Intuitive Connection

With the hope of midwinter's building light, and Capricorn's drive to create social order, the intuitive mind is opened—to connect with friends, large groups and organizations to formulate an array of revolutionary resolutions! This mental connection with others, sparks the imaginations in all participants!

HOUSE #12: PISCES ~ Completion

In this final month in the cycle, the actions that we contributed six months ago in Virgo's House of Service, will now bring their rewards. What we have given, will now be received with greater returns.

This House contains all subjects and thoughts that support one's feelings of purpose and wholeness. Here, we also find the impact of our "failure to serve others". It will be the Karma, that every person will carry forward, when he or she begins the new creative adventure—that begins in the Spring!

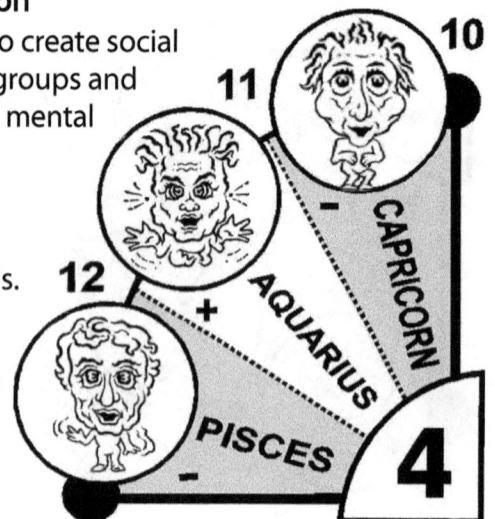

Ruling Planets and Houses

As the ancients watched the transits of the planets and luminaries, they discovered that their placement (in a certain segment of their charts) would increase the impact of the component. With this, each of the planets were given their own assigned House (or sector in the chart) to rule!

Originally, to fill the extra Houses, the inner planets **Mercury**, **Venus** and **Mars** were assigned duel rulerships. **Jupiter** and **Saturn** also were duel rulers in Houses 9 thru 12. With the discovery of **Neptune**, **Uranus** and **Pluto**, they took rulership of Houses 8, 11 and 12. The graphic shows how these rulers fit into the 12 Houses in the chart.

It is significant that the ancients placed the homes for the luminaries and four personal planets in the *lower daylight portion of the wheel*--for this is where individuals learn to perform the functions and actions of their "**Sun**-lit" personal needs. **Mercury** activates the bicameral mind; **Venus** delights and arouses the physical senses. **Mars** ignites the fire of our desires, while the **Moon** reflects the ebb and crest of our emotions.

In the upper hemisphere of the chart, **Venus** finds its 2nd rulership in **Libra**, as it joins the five **transpersonal planets** in the *Other Half* of the year. The lengthy cycles of these outer planets are more difficult to observe and track, and therefore, their influences are not as obvious as the personal planets. However, they allow us to map the long-range trends in a person's life.

Houses and Rulers for the 12 Signs

The illustration shows the symbols of the eight planets and two luminaries and the Houses they rule in the chart. Notably, the placement of any component in any House infuses the qualities of its ruler into the makeup of the component. For example: A Saturn conjunction can slow down the mercuric nature of a Gemini Sun. If Jupiter, it becomes more animated.

In all personal charts, the Sign that was "rising on the eastern horizon" at one's time of birth, becomes the First House in the chart. This starting point, and the Sign on the Ascendant, greatly dictates the appearance that one presents to others. *(See celebrities who share common Ascendants, on page 65.)*

The Nature of the Planets

The influence of the planets often reflect the nature of their physical makeup. For instance, **Jupiter** is our solar system's largest planet. With this "largeness", Jupiter brings expansion and the unrestrained qualities that are associated with the unrestrained and expansive fire of **Sagittarius**.

All the while, **Saturn** is the last planet that can be physically seen by the naked eye. Thusly, this ringed planet became the

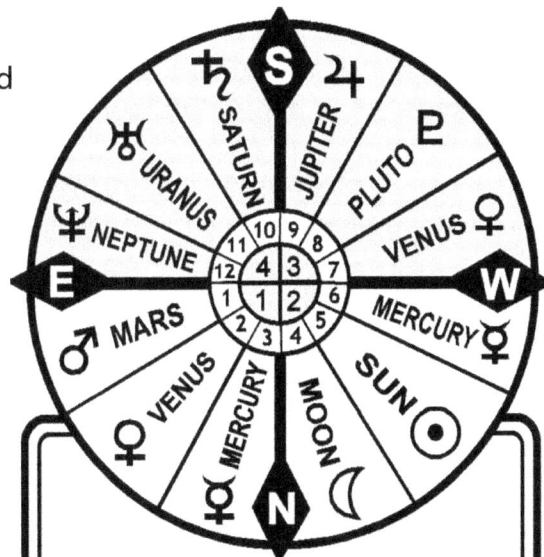

Houses / Planets / Signs

#1: ♂ **MARS** *rules* **ARIES** ♈

2/7: ♀ **VENUS** *rules the signs:* **TAURUS** ♉ & **LIBRA** ♎

3/6: ☿ **MERCURY** *rules* **GEMINI** ♊ & **VIRGO** ♍

4: ☽ **MOON** *rules* **CANCER** ♋

5: ☉ **SUN** *rules* **LEO** ♌

8: ♇ **PLUTO = SCORPIO** ♏

9: ♃ **JUPITER** *rules* **SAG** ♐

10: ♄ **Saturn** rules **Capricorn** ♑

11: ♅ **Uranus** rules **Aquarius** ♒

12: ♆ **Neptune** rules **Pisces** ♓

ruler of **Capricorn**, the Sign that is associated with physical limits and restrictions.

The planet **Neptune** is a mix of "icy" fluids —water, methane and ammonia. The Greek God Neptune is the lord of the oceans—and the home of the **Pisces** fish.

Uranus is colder and more distant, and it is assigned as the ruler of **Aquarius**.

On the outer edge of our biosphere, lies tiny **Pluto**—the new planet assigned to rule the mysterious Sign of **Scorpio**.

All of these planets and luminaries appear to run in synch with each other, and each one's position affects all of the others.

The physical impact of these aspects are demonstrated on page 76.

The Key Components in the chart

After years of viewing the daily, monthly and yearly cycles in the heavens, astrologers came to recognize that there were six primary components—that were effecting the personality, appearance and emotional natures of their family and friends. The most important of these "personal components" are the three luminescent colorings of the **Sun**, the **Moon** and the **Ascendant**. They are supported and augmented by the rhythmical cycles in the Three Personal Planets: **Mercury**, **Venus** and **Mars**.

The Yearly Cycle: ☉ The Sun

The Fire and Source of Light, Radiant Energy, Projection, Self-Expression, Leo, The Fifth House, The Creative Spirit

The primal element of any image-making process is LIGHT! It is the bounce of light, that gives an image its illusion of form. Without light, there no movie to see. No great projector in the sky!

In this big cosmic drama, the light on our planet comes from the Sun. It is the governor of the seasons, the god of agriculture and guardian of herds and flocks—and the source of all light creations on this Earth!

Your Sun Sign is the most important factor in your horoscope. Just as the Sun inspires the creation of all life on this Earth, it also *lights up your world*! The angle of the Earth to the Sun determines the radiance, color and magnetic nature of your individual self expressions. It is the force you project out to others! The area in which these solar forces land, is defined by the Sun's location (or House) in the chart.

These solar rays give you the desire to replicate and emulate the purpose, function and creative qualities that were occurring in the month and season, in which you were born. The mode and element of your Sun Sign determines the nature of the your actions, and how you project your desires to others. These solar expressions may be redefined by your other components, and the aspects that they make to your Sun.

When people age and grow into fullness, they become more capable of exhibiting the qualities of their Suns. Many become more creative, generous, big hearted and magnanimous—all positive solar traits! Sadly, who fail to express their true solar nature, often attempt to dim the "lights" of others.

☉ The Sun rules the Sign of Leo; ♌ Leo rules the 5th House

Everything evolves around the ball of fire that is at the center of our solar system. Perhaps that is why so many Lions feel that *everything evolves around them!* This desire to be on center stage can be attributed to the fixed and "self-focused fire" of Leo, and it is why theater and show biz are both ruled by the Sign of Leo. Positively, these lion gifts inspire all of us to "shine" our inner light—and project the solar qualities that we were given on our day of birth.

The Sun lights up the field, where you stand.

With the changing Ascendant, the Sun can be located in any House in the chart. When we know the House where our Sun resides, it tells us of the arena or field in life, **WHERE** we can express our creative desires and distinguish ourselves from others. If the Sign on the cusp of the House is in a different sign than one's Sun Sign, one's field of pursuit is likely a combination of the two. Aspects to the Sun, reveal the insights and special talents that one was given, to support his or her solar desires. Add them all together, and you get the amazing assemblage of colored lights—that is YOU!

The 5th House is where your creativity finds a home.

In the order of the Signs, Leo is 5th in line. Therefore, Leo becomes the ruler of the 5th House.

The Sign on your 5th House cusp often indicates **HOW** you approach, pursue and apply the creative urges of your Sun. The manner in which you create (to define your sense of individuality) is described in the 5th House. These creative activities may tilt to the arts, sports, romantic relationships, and more. It is further clarified by the Sign of the planets in the 5th House. Often, we will find that a person with Neptune in the 5th house will find recognition in the arts—music, poetry, visual arts and acting. For those with an aspect between Neptune and Mercury, the music will be felt in the poetry of their words.

The Monthly Cycle: ☽ The Moon

Reflection of Light, Reactive Energy, Subconsciousness, Emotional Memory, Nurturing Mother, Cancer, Fourth House

In the dark of night, the Moon reflects the rays of the Sun back to Earth. In every sidereal month or lunar cycle, the Moon transits thru the 12 Zodiac Signs—changing Signs every 2.5 days! This Moon's entrance into the next Sign chances an individual's emotional state and attitude, but it has little physical effect.

Your Moon was transiting a certain Sign on the day of your birth. This Sign (and the nature of its Mode and Element) indicates **how** you internalize and react to the incoming light, that you receive from others. These instinctual feelings tell you HOW to find emotional comfort and security in your surroundings.

Previously, the Sun became the projector in our personal movie theater. The Moon is the silver screen, that reflects a person's personal reactions —out to others! The Sign of the Moon defines the nature of our emotional reactions. It tells us where we find comfort (mostly in our homes). The Moon's Element and Mode tells us how we react to joy, surprise and bad news.

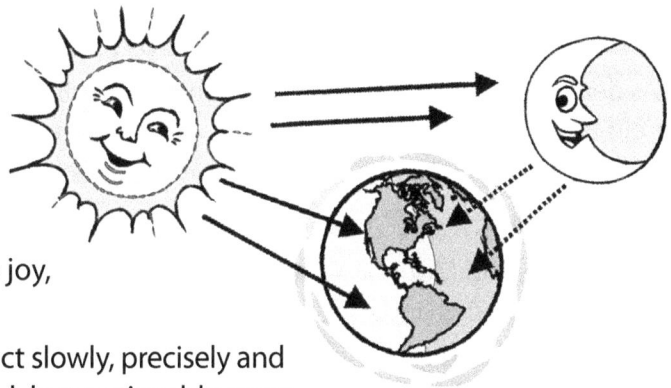

If one's Moon is in a **Earth** Sign, he/she tends to react slowly, precisely and deliberately. If a **Water** Moon, they are also reserved, but noticeably more fluid and emotional. In contrast, a **Fire** Sign Moon brings quick and sharp reactions. **Air** Sign Moons are noticeably mental and electrical in their responses. With a **Cardinal Moon**, their reactions are strongly directed. **Fixed Moons** are notably hesitant or resistant to react, while **Mutable Moons** consistently jump from one emotional attachment to another.

These shifting tides of reflected light draw out our favorite memories, and what we emotionally hold to be dear. What is "memorable" is defined by the nature of the Sign of one's Moon. **Gemini Moons** recall the moments, when their complicated ideas found new solutions. **Leo Moons** seem to remember the romantic and theatrical moments, when they felt true love (and/or adulation) from others. **Virgo Moons** become mercuric and emotional, when their services are recognized by others. **Pisces Moons** seem to be remember all of their emotional experiences at the same time. Do your emotional reactions and favorite memories match the Sign in which your Moon is placed?

[Photos of celebrities who share common Moon Signs begin on page 60.]

☽ The Moon rules the Sign Cancer; Cancer rules the 4th House ♋

When the Sun reaches its highest peak at the **Summer Solstice**, there is a major redirection—as the Sun begins its six month, downward journey into the darkness of **Winter**. With this dimming light, the Cancer Crab settles into her protective shell on the bottom of the sea. But there, the Moon is shifting the tides everyday. This lack of security compels the Crab, to seek a permanent base of comfort! This base of comfort is found in the **4th House** in the chart. This is why the **Moon** became the ruler of the Sign of **Cancer**.

The Sign on the 4th House Cusp defines **how** we relate to our homes and family. I.E., folks with **Aries** on the cusp often feel independent from their families, and their homes are often, just a place to sleep.

The House, where one's Moon is placed reveals **where** one seeks his/her emotional fulfillment. I.E., people with their Moons in Gemini's **House #3** find emotional delight, intellectualizing data and communicating with others. In contrast, those with their Moons in their Taurus-ruled **House#2** are emotionally separated from others. It is the "stuff" in their surroundings that give them their feelings of comfort.

The Dance of the Primal Lights
How the Sun and Moon Light Up the Personality

To clarify the importance of the two luminaries, let us now look at how the Sun's projecting rays and the Moon's reflecting beams operate in unison, to shape and define a person's personality.

When people project their solar light and then respond with their lunar reactions—we get the primary mechanism-of-animation, that defines the **psyche**—or the psycho-dynamics in their personalities. The nature of the dynamics are determined by the Signs in which a person's Sun and Moon are placed.

Using groups of the modes and elements, we will show how these two primal lights define the manner in how a people projects and interacts with others. The character of these actions may be altered by the placement and aspects of the other planets in one's charts, and also by the current transits of the planets—most noticeably by the Moon.

Luminaries in the Same Mode

As described earlier, the modes are the "patterning forces" that drive, meld and change all creations. Here are examples of celebrities who have both of their luminaries in the same Mode.

Sarah Jessica Parker, *Cardinal Sun and Moon:*

With a Sun and Moon in Cardinal Signs, Sarah's personality is highly driven, impetuous and emotionally tenacious.

Sarah's **Aries Sun** gives her the instant impulses, the fiery temper and the seemingly unstoppable drive that she displayed in "*Sex in the City*". Her solar fires are countered by her earthy, rugged and cool **Capricorn Moon** reactions. Watch how she switches from fire to earth, when she projects her Sun, and then reacts to others.

William J. Clinton, *Fixed Sun and Moon:*

The previous "urge to GO" grinds to a STOP, when the Fixed Signs take control. The fixed sense of confidence of Bill Clinton's **Leo Sun** shined brightly, when he was on stage. He also was known for his long-winded descriptions of physical details—that seemed to go on forever.

This fixation on detail was likely a product of his earthy Venus-ruled **Taurus Moon**. This verbosity was spread by Clinton's five components in airy and cardinal **Libra**, the other Sign that is ruled by Venus.

Next, to break the pattern of HOLD, let's give things a whole new spin and inject the force of mutability:

Ben Stiller, *Mutable Sun and Moon*

Expect big changes when this fiery **Sagittarius** gallops into the room. His Mutable Fire always keeps things in an excited whirl, as he fills the room with joy and laughter.

However, watch how this Centaur suddenly becomes bewildered and filled with doubt—when the emotional waters of his **Pisces Moon** rise up, to douse his Sun's fire. This juxtaposition from "unbridled enthusiasm to emotional insecurity" defines the pattern that made his comedic work so enjoyable.

Luminaries in the Same Element

Next, we will show what happens, when both luminaries are placed in a common Element. With both luminaries in the same Element, the quality or force of these celebrity's expressions does not change. We only see alterations in the modal patterns in their actions.

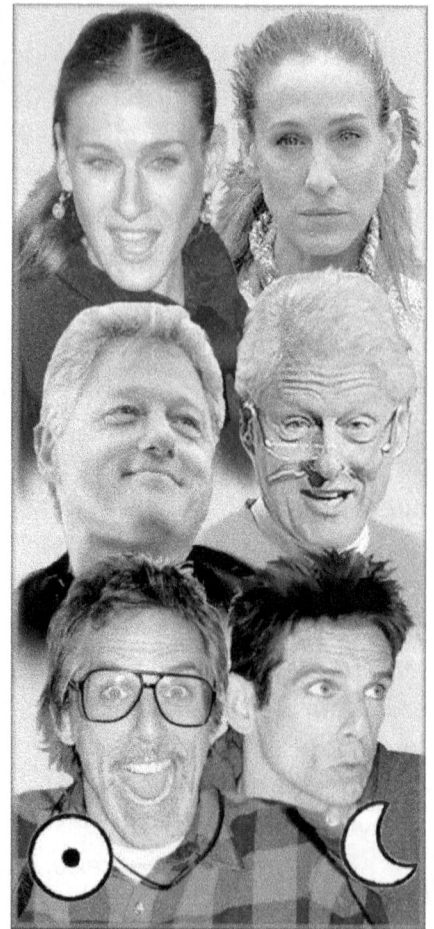

Celine Dion, *Sun and Moon in Fire Signs*

The intense force of fire is seen in this triple Fire Sign. With her **Sun** and **Moon** in fiery **Aries**, and a **Leo Ascendant**, Dion turns up the heat, when she performs on state.

The Fire of her Cardinal Sun and Moon gives her a strong sense of direction, intense expressions and instant reactions. With Mars on her Aries Moon trine Jupiter *, her emotional reactions are succinct, sharp and to the point.   [* See page 76 for more details on aspects.]

Gene Wilder, *Sun and Moon in Air Signs*

Here, the expansive energies are not as intense as Fire. Rather, they are lighter and more breezy. Wilder's **Gemini Sun** and **Aquarius Moon** is giving his expressions and reactions the flighty qualities of Air.

When Gene flies into a room, watch how his Gemini hands fan the air and his feet barely touch the ground. His vaporous and breezy personality is enhanced by the fixed air reactions of his Aquarius Moon. These intuitive flashes and outrageous surprises keep things in a whirl.

Will Ferrell, *Sun and Moon in Water Signs*

Watch how the Cardinal Waters of Ferrell's **Cancer Sun** pull his bulging facial flesh sharply to the side, and how—with every emotional change, the tidal wave turns the bulge in the other direction.

Ferrell is not the typical timid Crab, his erratic mannerisms are a product of Uranus and Pluto's conjunction on his **Virgo Ascendant** and *their sextile to his* **Scorpio Moon**. Watch how his emotions shift from being erratic and fussy and then suddenly intensely controlling. This shows how planet placements can change the energy of one's Moon and Sun.

George Clooney, *Sun and Moon in Earth Signs*

The most solid in any grouping, would be those with luminaries made of Earth. Thusly, Clooney appears to be the "rock" of this bunch.

Watch how his fixed **Taurus Sun** keeps him locked in the *here and now*, contentedly enjoying life's physical pleasures. This grounded and sensual nature us embellished by his tenacious **Capricorn Moon**. This Moon makes him emotionally cautious, while its conjunction to Saturn and Jupiter accounts for the delightfully entertaining DRY wit and coolness, that we saw in his *Oceans 11+* films.

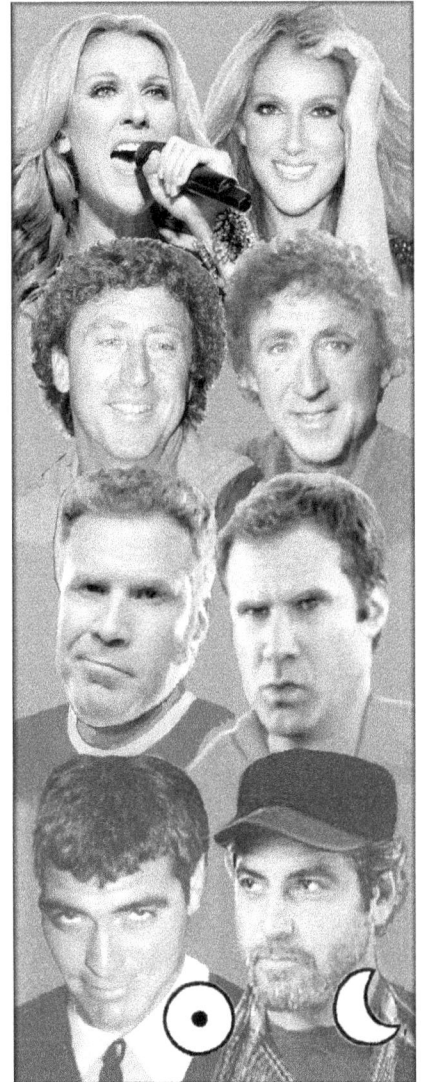

This rigid image is loosened by the Mutable Water of his **Pisces Ascendant**. Its trines his Neptune and sextiles Pluto. This gives him the dreamy and seductive persona, that makes him so appealing to others.

On page 76, the *Snapshots* of **Renee Zellweger** and **Jack Nicholson** demonstrate the mannerisms of two Taurus Suns, who have strong Leo—and also powerful Pluto or Neptune connections.

Many Renderings of Light

With these two luminaries, there is the potential of combining twelve Sun Signs with twelve different Moon Signs. This alone, gives us a potential of 144 combinations of Elements and Modes.

When the Ascendant, three personal planets (Mercury, Venus and Mars) and the other five outer planets are added in—and the aspects between them are considered—*the possibilities become incredible!*

Next, we look at those other components in the chart, and show how they affect the personality.

25

The Ascendant

The Mask & Physical Body; The 1st House & One's View to the World

In their watching of the Northern sky at night, the ancients saw that different groups of stars would appear near the setting Sun on the West horizon, and then move CCW in a their regular order--to appear in pre-dawn light six hours later, on the **Eastern Horizon**. With this, they determined that a different Sign would rise in the morning light every two hours.. With this, they could calculate the Sign that was rising in the East at anyone's moment of birth. This became the person's Rising Sign, or Ascendant.

In dawn's early light, the meaning of the moment is defined

Unlike the ancients, today we know that it is the Earth's daily CCW rotation on its axis that determines the time and place of Sunrise on the Earth. We also know that the Sun remains in a Sign for an average duration of 30.43 days—and with the Earth's daily CCW rotation, the Rising Sign on the Eastern horizon moves to the West one degree every 4 minutes, and it changes Signs every two hours, and far less at extreme latitudes. Also, as **Earth rotates CCW**, this rising point brings a **New Day** to a different longitude line on the Earth.

As noted previously, it is the **Earth's axis tilt,** that explains the Sun's daily rise and fall in the sky, and why the Sun reaches its highest point in the Summer and its lowest point in the Winter.

Since the Ascendant pinpoints one's *physical place* of birth, it defines the *physical frame* in one's body, and the bone structure in a person's face. The Rising Sign is seen in the face, when a person's facial flesh is not animating its solar or lunar qualities. Resting in repose, the face takes on the contours of the underlying skeletal formations. This becomes "the physical mask" that others see on first impression.

For centuries, astrologers have said that **"The Rising Sign starts the clock in every person's chart".** This is supported by today's "seasonal biologists", who claim that our Circadian and body biorhythms all "start at zero" at our moment of birth. Oddly, many of these scientists insist that "they have nothing to do with astrology". The big question is: "Why do they refuse to study the history of the work, that was the origin of their science?"

When the Sun's rays are focused, Light come into viewable form

In our "movie analogy", the Sun and Moon are the projector and the screen. The Ascendant becomes the lens, that focuses the transmitted light into viewable form. Since light runs both ways through this lens, the Ascendant defines how a person is seen by others, and it also shapes how he/she sees the world.

A **Taurus Ascendant** would suggest a lens equal to the human eye—where one sees the real world, as it is interpreted by one's senses! **Scorpio Rising**'s microscope sees the smaller, hidden secrets. A **Sagittarius Ascendant** implies the use of a wide-angle lens, that brings a giant range of things into view! **Aquarius Rising** suggests the telescope, the device that brings distant images in space into view.

Since the Ascendant sets the Signs on all of the Houses in the chart, it also colors the way that a chart owner is likely to approach each House's intent. For instance, folks who have Aries on their 4th House cusp will rarely be at home. Those with Gemini on the 7th House will seek a partner who is a great conversationalist. The Signs on the Houses tell each chart owner the directions, that he/she must take, to fulfill one's destiny.

See Celebrities with common Ascendants on page 65.
*Or check out the Sun, Moon and Ascendants of the **24 Celebrity Snapshots**, that begin on page 84.*

The Daily Movement of the Sun, as it appears in the sky

To understand the role of the Ascendant in the chart, it is important to understand how the daily rotation of the Earth and the Sun's daily rise and fall in the sky changes the Signs on the Eastern horizon. This enables us to estimate anyone's Ascendant, without math or a computer. For simplicity's sake, we are using the Rising Sign of a **Cancer Sun** lady, **born near the solstice** (June 25) *at high Noon* in **Sacramento, CA.**

We know that *the Sun always rises in the same Sign in which it is placed*, therefore, our subject will have Cancer Rising at daybreak. In the city of Sacramento, the Sun rises around 6 A.M. on that date (*Circle 1*).

Google with tell you the time of sunrise on any date, in any city.

Moving towards to her Noon birth time, we place 9 A.M. (**Circle 2**) on the Eastern horizon. There, the Earth's CCW rotation on its axis places the Sun somewhere in the mid-Pacific Ocean. There, the Sun is still in Cancer, but **Leo** or **Virgo** is rising on the eastern horizon.

With another 2 hour spin of the wheel, the Earth's tilt places the Cancer Sun near its "Noon point" in the sky (*Circle 3*). With this, **Libra is rising** somewhere just west of Asia. Our subject's Ascendant is likely Libra.

This series of circled numbers shows how the Earth's spin moves the original Sun's position (#1) to the east—while the Earth's axis tilt moves it to the north, until it reaches its highest point at Noon. *(See axis tilt, page 9.]* In all this, the Sun does not move; Nor does one's birth spot on the globe, but the rotating Earth creates a new Rising Sign in the East, every 2 hours or so. This time is shortened or extended, depending on one's latitudes.

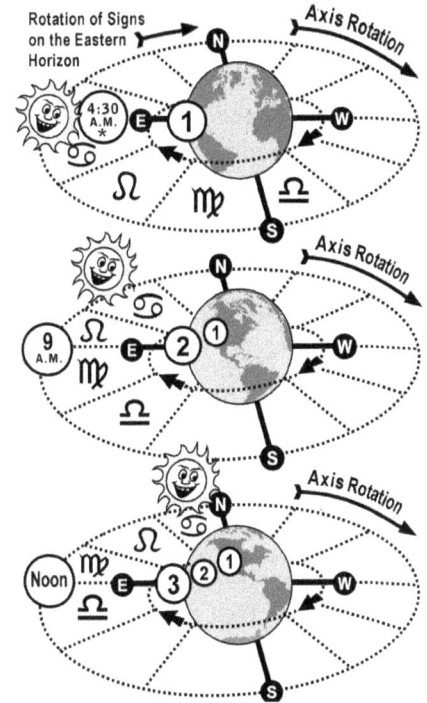

How to estimate a person's Ascendant

If the birth time is unknown, but you were told "the part of the day when the subject was born", it is fairly easy to ballpark one's Ascendant. Begin by sketching a rough "24 Hour Clock", that will place your subject's *Sun and Sunrise on the left side of the clock*. Next, in order, *place the other signs of the SAME MODE* on the Noon, Sunset & Midnight hours on the clock. With this, you can guess his/her time of birth.

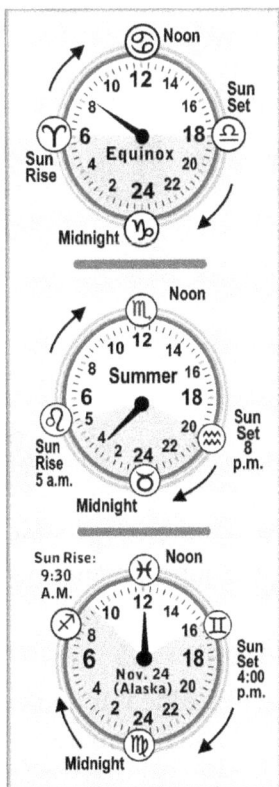

The 1st clock shows the **Spring Equinox**, a season of equal Days and Nights. With our subject being an **Aries Sun Sign**, Aries is placed on the left and the other Cardinal Signs are placed on the 3 other key hour points. If he thinks that he was born "in the pre-noon hours", we know that his Ascendant will be Aries. Taurus, Gemini or Cancer. Check his physical features and made your guess. *(This technique of using physical traits to guess one's Ascendant is explained on page 78).*

The 2nd clock is set for a **Leo** lady, who states she was born on August 2, *"between midnight and before dawn."* With that, we placed **Leo** on the point of sunrise (5 A.M.), and the other Fixed Signs on the other compass points. **Write in the times** that you googled, to capture midsummer's hours of sunrise, high noon, sunset and midnight.

Between midnight and sunrise, this lady will have **Taurus**, **Gemini**, **Cancer** or **Leo** rising. If she has square and cubical features and they appear "bovine in nature", she could be Taurus Rising. If she shows skewed facial lines, she is likely Gemini Rising. If she shows the round lunar temples of the crab, she is likely born around 4 A.M. If born near sunrise, the features of a Lion should be obvious. If none of these fit, check for planets on the Sun or Ascendant. They may be altering her appearance.

The 3rd clock is for an early degree **Sagittarius**, born on November 24 "during the day light hours" in Anchorage, Alaska. On this date at Latitude 60 degrees North, the Sun rises at 9:30 A.M. and sets at 4:00 P.M. Here, the other Mutable Signs are placed on the 4 key hours on the clock. In this location's 6.5 hours of daylight, seven of the 12 Signs are passing over the eastern horizon. In cases like this, try to narrow down the hours of birth time, by using the lessons in this book to identify the traits of the Signs.

~ The Personal Planets ~

MERCURY
The Messenger, The Thinking Process, Initial Conceptualizing of Ideas

In ancient times, Mercury was the *Winged Messenger of the Gods,* and it is why astrologers assigned the planet Mercury to rule our thinking process—and the way we think, short and gather in data.

Some believe that the light of the Sun is bent by Mercury's gravitational fields—and somehow, Mercury's orbit changes the oscillating voltages in the human brain. But whatever the reason, the Sign and House of Mercury captures the nature of a person's **mental biorhythms**. It affects us all, when Mercury goes retrograde.

With its closeness to the Sun, Mercury can only occupy the Sign of the Sun or one of the Signs on either side. Thusly, half of us will have Mercury in the same Sign as our Sun; The other half may their Mercury in a differently polarized sign. Those with a positively-charged Mercury and a receptively-charged Sun, will often find that their minds run faster than their Sun's capability to express words and language. (In reverse, it's the opposite).

Mercury defines the device, that records the data

In our movie making analogy, Mercury is "the camera" that captures the sound and images in a movie. Some cameras run fast, capturing shorter moments of time. Those with high speed film record scenes with little light. In today's digital world, different devices give us different speeds and amounts of memory. Perhaps, Mercury could also be the software, that operates these computations? Mercury also symbolizes the treatment, or the simple outline of a script, that diagrams the concepts in any movie. In the making, Mercury would be the single "take"— that out of a series of many—will make up a scene in the final program. Any artistic adjustments become the task of *Venus.*

Associations: Mercury is the ruler of Gemini and Virgo, the analyzers of the Zodiac. The House in which your Mercury is placed, represents the area of expertise and the subject material, that you will find to be "the easiest to compile and analyze". Houses 3 and 6 are the natural homes of Gemini and Virgo.

Effects of Mercury and its Rulership

To clarify this concept (and to give us insight into the impact of Mercury), here we show how the Mercury-ruled signs of Gemini and Virgo Suns are affected by the placement of Mercury. With its rulership of these two Signs, this planet's placement distinctly alters the nature of their "Mercuric Suns".

Charlie Sheen: Virgo Sun, Mercury in Leo (9/3/1965)

Charlie shows few of Virgo's worrisome and nervous qualities. Rather, he often appears over confident and self assured. Mercury, the ruling planet of his Sun, is in the Fixed Fire Sign of Leo. Sheen's earthy and mutable Sun gives him the fussy qualities associated with Virgo. However, these mercuric solar qualities are often overridden by the self-aggrandizing and theatrical thoughts of his Leo Mercury. He once thought that he had "tiger blood" in his veins.

Morgan Freeman: Gemini Sun, Mercury in Taurus (6/1/1937)

Judging from his earthy voice, and his steady accumulation of rock solid creative works, many of us wouldn't expect Morgan Freeman to be a Gemini.

Mutable Air Signs are suppose to be flighty, highly animated and extremely talkative. In most of his roles, Freeman's words and thoughts flowed slowly and steadily. His mind never seems to be in a hurry, and neither is his "thought driven" Sun. His Mercury is in the Fixed Earth Sign of Taurus,

Enhancement of the mind, brings the beauty of Venus

With Mercury's input, we are given an array of wonderful ideas. The next step is to group those ideas together into greater concepts. This creative desire begins, when our Mercury thoughts are refined and harmoniously arranged by Venus, the second of the three personal planet. It is the physical, emotional, mental and spiritual creations of Venus that *make us happy!*

VENUS
Enhancement of Mind, Art Refinement, Feminine Attraction (The Anima), What Makes You Happy

For the ancient Greeks, Aphrodite was the Goddess of Love, who showed mortals the importance of beauty, romance, adoration and partnerships. For astrologers, Venus represents the value that we put on material objects. In physiological terms, Venus defines how one relates to others.

Venus is the ruler of two Signs: **Taurus** and **Libra**. *Receptive Taurus* represents the feminine creative principle of Carl Jung's **Anima**—the unconscious femininity in a person's psyche, that *attracts others to one's self*. Meanwhile, *masculine-charged Libra* suggests Jung's **Animus**—or the masculine side of a person that is *projected outward*—to makes one's self *appealing to others*. Your Venus Sign often indicates what you seek in your intimate relationships. Its House of placement suggests the type of people you will attract in your business and social partnerships.

Venus designs the sets and costumes, aims the lights and directs the movie!

With Mercury's script in hand, it is time to create a movie! The physical props will be constructed by workers with Venus in Taurus. Further contributions will come from others, who will use the skills of their Venus, to share their creative ideas with others.

Any movie director's main vision may be the expression of his or her lifelong solar desires, but when the creative calls are made (be it the tone of the actor's voice, the coloring of the light, or the composition in the frame), the director's final artistic choice is often shaped and defined by the nature of the Sign in which his or her Venus is placed.

Not sure of someone's Venus? Check out their rooms and clothing. A lot of oceanic blues suggests a love of water. Add some yellow and make the blue lighter, and their Venus is likely in Air. Reds and oranges indicate Fire. Brown and green tones are the stuff of Earth.

The House where Venus is placed indicates the area of your life where "your artistic urges desire to create harmony". Venus functions well in the homes of Taurus and Libra, since they are ruled by Venus.

Effects of Venus, and its Rulership

With these Venus-ruled Sun Sign celebrities, we show how the placement of their Venus alters their creative impulses:

TAURUSES: Tina Fey, Orson Welles (Venus in Gemini and Aries)

Tina Fey (5/18/1970) was head writer and performer on "*Saturday Night Live*" and writer/producer/actress for "*30 Rock*". Tina's Sun is ruled by **Venus**, but her Venus is in **Gemini**! This placement kicks her mind into overdrive, as she creates a prolific flow of words and ideas. This is unusual for a Taurus Sun.

Orson Welles (5/6/1915) was one of Hollywood's most driven film directors. His film "*Citizen Kane*", completed when he was only 29, is considered by many to be the greatest film of all time. This youthful drive and unstoppable creative force is often seen in folks who have a **Venus in Aries**.

LIBRAS: Julie Andrews, Deepak Chopra (Venus in Virgo & Sagittarius)

Julie Andrews (10/01/1935) was the star of "*Sound of Music*" and other feel good movies. Recall the scene in "*Mary Poppins*", where she was joyfully singing, while cleaning the kitchen. This meticulous and proper force was apparent in her creative projects. That's what you see when a **Virgo Venus** goes to work.

Deepak Chopra (10/22/1946) is known for his "New Age" interpretation of health and spirituality. In his Sun's presentation, Libra's mental energies are quietly spoken and subdued by his *Pisces Ascendant*. Notably, his creative gifts are grand in scope and holistically oriented, for they are richly embellished by the spiritual insights of his **Sagittarius Venus**.

MARS
Physical Energy, Metabolism, The Animus, Masculine Projection (What makes you angry)

Mars was the God of War, the martial warrior who conquered others with physical force. When the ancients saw that the cycles of Mars were replicating the ups-and-downs in their friend's metabolism, they decreed that Mars would be the ruler of a person's physical drive. Contemporary scientists define these cycles as our "physical biorhythms".

If *Mercury* shows how we think, and *Venus* shows how we arrange *Mercury*'s thoughts to create something of value—then *Mars* will show us **how** we actually perform such physical tasks. Its House of placement tells us **where** these energies will be directed.

Mars determines the speed and strength of our physical metabolism. Some individuals run at higher speed, but don't have the torque or power of others. Others have strength, but little finesse. The quality of this muscular power is defined by the Sign in which Mars is placed.

The red planet Mars is associated with the red blood in our veins, that carries the nutrients, iron and oxygen to our bodies—to provide physical strength! Our blood also feeds the adrenaline, that flows *when we are angry*.

Mars tells us of the force that a person takes, to perform any physical action. The best way to determine one's Mars is to watch them at work. Don't take the first impression or any of their attempts at communication. Watch them for several minutes and observe *how they physically move*—when they are performing a physical task! Is it a holding pattern, meandering or a straight forward drive? (Fixed, Mutable or Cardinal?) Do they move with the intensity of fire? Are their actions sludgy, liquid or vaporous in nature? Put the mode and element together and you'll likely identify the Sign of an individual's Mars.

Associations: Mars is the ruler of Aries and the ancient ruler of Scorpio.

Mars was the ancient ruler of Aries and Scorpio. Today, Pluto is the ruler of Scorpio. The House where Mars is placed, indicates the area in one's life, where one's physical efforts will be directed. Some believe that Mars' natal placement (and its angle to the Ascendant), defines the cycle of a person's physical biorhythms.

Effects of Mars, and its Rulership

Here, we look at how the placement of Mars alters the expressive manners, the physical force and the creative drive of three **Aries Sun** comedians.

Eddie Murphy: Mars in Cancer (4/3/1961, Brooklyn, NY)

Early on, Eddie was successful in action films like *"Beverly Hills Cop"*. It's what you'd expect from an **Aries Sun**. However, with his Mars positioned in Cancer, Murphy's interest in action movies quickly faded—as his interest in family-oriented films blossomed. With the soft "force of Cancer", Eddie performed in family films like *"Nutty Professor"*, *"Dr. Doolittle"* and the lovable *"Shrek"*.

Paul Reiser, Mars in Gemini (3/30/1957, New York, NY)

With Sun, Moon, Mercury and Venus in **Aries**, you would expect Reiser to be a fully charged Ram. True, he is highly directed and successful at starting his own projects, but his "work" shows the energy and mental gymnastics of a **Gemini Mars.**

In his movie role in *"Diner"* and in his TV show *"Mad About You"*, the dynamics of Paul's Gemini Mars were revealed in his mercuric and animated gestures, and in his prolific outpouring of words. They never seemed to stop.

Martin Short, Mars in Libra (3/26/1950, Hamilton, Canada)

Martin's **Mars** is in **Libra**, opposing his **Aries** Sun and squaring his **Cancer** Moon. These aspects and the vacillating force of his Libra Mars, make it difficult for this triple Cardinal Sign to direct his energies in a single direction. In addition, Uranus' T-square to his Sun and Mars makes this movements erratic and unsettling.

In *"The Three Amigos"*, *"Father of the Bride"* and *"Prime Time Glick"*, Martin gave us characters who were unnerving, overly aggressive and abrasive—and seemingly desperate to "be friends with everyone he met". This Aries Sun (and his heavily aspected Mars) shows us that comedy isn't always pretty.

Previously, we showed how the Modal and Elemental qualities of the Sign, in which one's components are placed, defines the key layers in one's personality. The force and nature of this expression can be most easily see in the positioning and movements in a person's eyes.

The "Eyes" have it!

The eyes are the window to the soul, for they show the nature of the "lights" that were implanted at one's moment of birth. The Sun's nature is seen when a person is projecting the light of his or her solar expressions out to others. The Moon's glow is seen in their emotional reactions, and the nature of the Rising Sign is seen in the moments when the Sun and Moon are inactive. Many begin their guessing of a person's three key components by watching the modal pattern and elemental force of movement, in their subject's eyes. For beginners, it is best to use this technique to guess a person's Sun Sign.

CARDINAL EYES are aimed in the 4 Cardinal Directions

The **Eyes of ARIES** are aimed directly **to the front.** This sweeps the sharp-edged lashes and brows upward and to the back. It creates the intense and fiery eyes of the Ram.

In contrast, **Libra's** smiling eyes, long lashes and pillowed eyelids drift from one side to the other. This horizontal balance instills a sense of calmness.

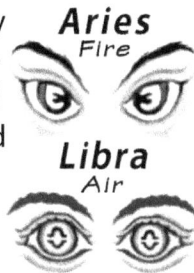

Aries Fire

Libra Air

Cancer Eyes *are always looking upward,* from their home on the the ocean floor below. These eyes are deeply encased, under the delta between the brows.
Capricorn eyes and craggy brows are aimed upward, as they scope the rugged trails, that will take them to distant mountain peaks.

Cancer Water

Capricorn Earth

FIXED EYES focus on outer and inner points

When they focus on the pleasures in their surroundings, the eyes and brows of **Taurus** are pulled downward and outward on the lower sides. This creates their Bovine eyes.

Scorpio's internally focused **Eyes** bend the brow, lids and pupils inward from the sides. This lifts the brows upward on the outer edges to give them their intense and hypnotic eyes

Taurus Earth

SCORPIO Water

Leo Eyes pull inward on the bottom. This sweeps them and the bushy brows upward and outward. The creates the eyes that we see in a Lion.

Aquarius' narrow-set **Eyes** are locked onto a distance point in space. This bends the brows in the center, as it pulls the hooded eyelids down on the outer sides.

LEO Fire

AQUARIUS Air

MUTABLE EYES skew off in different directions:

Watch how **Gemini's** right eye tilts above the left right, then quickly drops to place the left eye on the top. This positioning becomes obvious, when they're communicating their ideas to others.

The **horse Eyes** of **Sagittarius** flip from left to right, and their heads rear up and down—as they scan the path ahead.

Gemini Air

Sagittarius Fire

Watch how the squinted, thin lidded **Eyes** of **Virgo** twinkle, when they are handed a project to dissect and analyze.

When **Pisces Eyes** drift from side to side, the heavy lids drag one eye down from the other.

When the currents change, the other eye floats to the top again.

Virgo Earth

Pisces Water

Vedic astrologers believe that an individual's Sun rules the Right Eye—nd the left eye is ruled by one's Moon. To see how the aspects of Jupiter and Saturn distort the size of the eyes, see details on page 75.

How each Sign's rulership of a part of the body effects body language:

Another way to identify one's key components is to understand how each **Sign's rulership of a body part** affects a person's body language. This graphic shows how *3 Modes and 3 Signs* operate in each of the Four Quadrants in the body—and how all four work together, to fulfill key body functions and keep the body healthy!

Note how each quadrant starts with a Cardinal Sign and a Fixed Sign is placed in the center. The Mutable force (at the end of each quadrant) splits the field, as it spins into the next Cardinal section in the body—to begin the regulation of another body section.

The **1st Quadrant** contains *Aries'* Head, **Taurus'** neck and the lungs/hands of **Gemini**. Here, our cognitive, sensual and conceptual functions operate and interact with each other.

In **Quadrant 2**, **Cancer** begins the process of nourishing the body. **Leo 's Heart** distribute these nutrients (and Gemini's oxygen) to the body. Virgo digests the consumed nourishments, and feeds them to the various parts of the body.

Quadrant 3 is ruled by **Libra**, **Scorpio** and **Sagittarius**. In this part of the body, the kidney's filter out all valuables, and Scorpio eliminates the rest. Here, one *connect to other(s), to* create a greater esthetic, emotional and spiritual understanding of the outside world.

The **4th Quadrant** is the part where we find mobility, to move about in our world. Here, the **knees of Capricorn** activate our initial steps, to find a higher position in the world. In this pursuit, the **calves** of **Aquarius** send us skipping into new fields of exploration.

With the **meridians in the feet,** all of the body parts are connected, as **Pisces'** circulates the currents back to the head, to enclose the entire body in a unified torus field. That is why Pisces are considered to be the "Healers of the Zodiac".

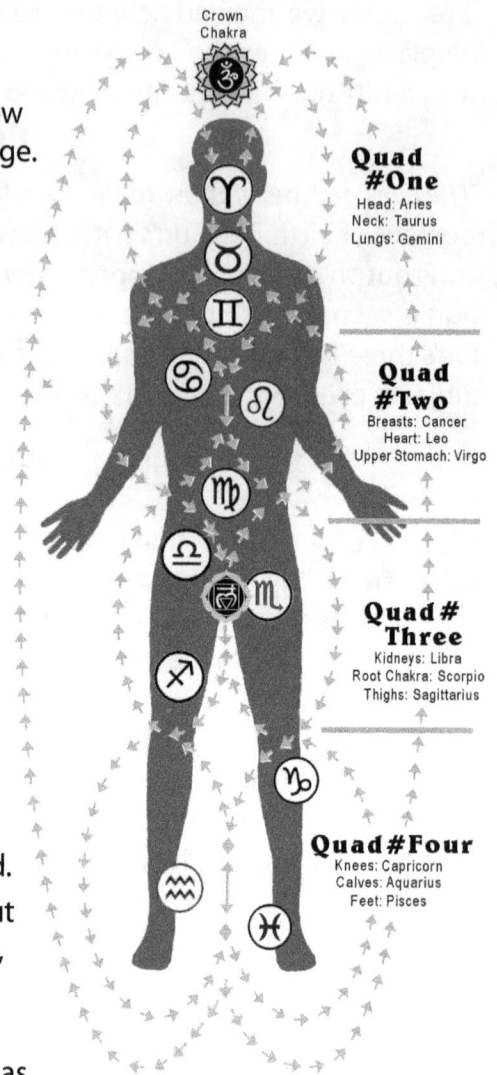

Crown Chakra

Quad #One
Head: Aries
Neck: Taurus
Lungs: Gemini

Quad #Two
Breasts: Cancer
Heart: Leo
Upper Stomach: Virgo

Quad # Three
Kidneys: Libra
Root Chakra: Scorpio
Thighs: Sagittarius

Quad #Four
Knees: Capricorn
Calves: Aquarius
Feet: Pisces

How a Sign's Rulership Affects Body Language:

Here, two celebrities show how *Aries' rulership of the head* and **Aquarius'** *rulership of the calves* activate different quadrants in the body. Unlike the exaggerated caricatures, this activity is very subtle. It is easiest to detect, when your subjects are moving, while exuberantly expressing their Solar natures.

Emma Watson shows us how the top quadrant of her body is fired up, when she initiates the cardinal fires of her **Aries Sun**. This placement in the head, tilts the head and the upper half of her body forward.

In contrast, **Justin Timberlake** shows how his **Aquarius Sun's** rulership of **the calves** leads the lower quadrant of his body to the front. This sends the upper torso, shoulders and head to the back.

Notably, Emma and Justin both have **Centaur Moons**. When emotionally interacting with others, their thighs are "fired up". Justin's legs lift higher as he become more animated. With Emma, her upper torso pulls back, as her thighs and legs spring to the front. This shows how our body language is constantly altered by our changing desires, thoughts and feelings.

32

Watch the Body Language of the Signs

The Body Language of Aries ~ Rules the Head & Eyes

Aries rules the Head and the Eyes. It is the Fire of Aries that provides the light that allows all to SEE the adventurous path that lies ahead. It is the Cardinal drive of this Sign, that drives individuals to **charge headfirst** down this path.

Sarah Jessica Parker shows us how the head of the Ram leads the way. Note the forward tilt of the head and how the upper half of her body leans to the front, as the feet trail to the rear.

Aries *Emma Watson* also shows Aries' head-strong stance, as also the militant posture of a Ram—ready to go on attack!

The Body Language of Taurus ~ Rules Neck & Shoulders

Taurus is the Zodiac Sign that follows Aries. Thusly, it is this Sign's Fixed Earth that empowers the next lower section in the body—i.e., the throat, neck and shoulders.

When you converse with your Taurus friends, note how their shoulders lean to the front. These heavy shoulders push the lower torso to the back. This bows the legs, as it plants the feet firmly on the ground.

Taurus Suns *Dwayne Johnson* and *Candice Bergman* show the focused eyes of Taurus, and how their heavy shoulders weigh to the front.

The Body Language of Gemini ~ Rules the Lungs & Arms

When rulership moves down into the hands, arms and lungs, this part of the body is electrified by the Mutable Air of Gemini. Note how the hands of your Gemini friends spin and swirl, as they disperse their array of ever changing thoughts.

Can we talk?

Joan Rivers

Dana Carvey

Body Language of Cancer ~ Rules the Breasts & Esophagus

On the Solstice, the Sun begins its downward journey in the sky. This shift in direction is seen in the upper chest of most Cancer Sun Signs, since this body part is ruled by this Cardinal Water Sign.

This forward trust of the chest shifts their shoulders sharply to the back, and it tilts the head sharply to the front. These Crabs have to look upward, to observe what lies in front of them. With their heavy torsos, every step tilts their body to that side. The next step tilts the torso in the opposite direction. What we see is the sideways shuffle of the Crab.

Linda Ronstad, Cheech Marin
Benedict Cumberbatch

Body Language of Leo ~ Rules the Heart

When these Lions strut into the room, the Fixed Fire expands the heart forward. This throws the shoulders and head upward, to create the prideful stance of the Lion. In the face, the bushy eyebrows pull down in the center, as the chin juts forward.

Leos: Mick Jagger, Jennifer Lawrence, Garrison Keillor

Body Language of Virgo ~ Rules the Stomach

With Virgo's rulership of the stomach, the force of Mutable Earth centers in the upper digestive track and the stomach. This protruding stomach pulls the chest to the back, as it tilts the head, shoulders and hips in opposing directions.

Bill Murray, Pink, Lily Tomlin

33

The Body Language of Libra ~ Rules the Head & Eyes

Here, in the *center of the body* (halfway between Aries' Head and Pisces' feet) the Cardinal Air of Libra is spreading the forces horizontally. This is why Libras desire to keep balance in their surroundings. This is also what we see in their body language.

As CEO of "Goop", *Gweneth Paltrow*'s Libra Sun supplies the world with an endless supply of her Venusian products—to make the world more beautiful. This "balanced posture" can also be seen in Libra *John Lennon*. Notably, he has Aries Rising. Yet, even when in a rush, his upper torso appears to be vertically balanced.

The Body Language of Scorpio ~ Rules the Pelvis Region

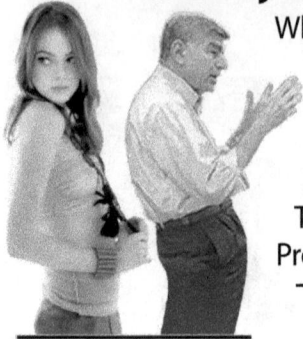

When rulership drops below the midpoint of the body, the power is anchored in the pelvis region of the body. Empowerment in this area trusts the hips to the front. This sends the torso tilting to the rear. To counter, the shoulders curve sharply forward, to align with the neck. This profile is seen in many Scorpio Suns and in those with a Scorpio Ascendant.

This easy-to-recognize body language is seen in former U.S. Presidential candidate *Michel Dukakis* and movie star *Emma Stone*.

Body Language of Sagittarius
~ Rules the Hip Joints & Thighs ~

When the Fire of Sagittarius is placed in the two thighs, the force is divided. This Mutable force empowers the two legs, and they enable the body to travel to distant points. These high-stepping thighs can be seen in the galloping Centaur. Watch how one step sends them in one direction; The next step aims them in the other. With this excitement, their Gemini arms will wave about and fan the fires, as they trot on by.

Dick Van Dyke
Bette Midler
Scarlett Johansson

Body Language of Capricorn ~ Rules the Knees

It is clear that the scattered fires of the Centaur need to be brought under control and given direction. This control comes in the knees, the body part ruled by Capricorn. Here, the Cardinal force maps out the direction, while Earth insures that each step will be cautiously and strategically placed. With this, the goat can complete its climb to the top of the Mountain.

Jude Law and *Greta Thunberg* show us their knees lead to the front, from the upper half of the body. This keeps them anchored on the Earth, as they move about their worlds.

Body Language of Aquarius ~ Rules the Calves

On top of the mountain, the mind is free—to fix onto higher goals. It is the Fixed Air of Aquarius that formulates these concepts, and it is the calves that enable all idealists to chase after their wildest ideas. Watch how their thighs fan the air, as they skip across the room, to greet and converse with their many friends. Oddly, each of these conversations will quickly end— as they bounce away—to engage in one with someone else.

Jackie Gleason

Harry Styles
Ellen DeGeneres

Body Language of Pisces ~ Rules the Feet

With Pisces rulership of the feet, the meridians in each foot are activated, to make their connections to all of the parts in the body. Your Pisces friends feel ALL of these connections; That's why they are the *Healers of the Zodiac*. ~~ Watch how the changing currents bob their heads, shoulders and hips up-and-down in opposite directions—as they paddle "feet first" down their paths of destiny!

Drew Barrymore, William Macy

The Zodiac Signs

With the basics of astrology completed, this book's proceeds to tie all of the previous data together, as it identifies the traits in each of the Sun Signs. It will then show how these primal Suns are reshaped by a person's Ascendant and Moon—and also changed by the aspects and degrees (decans and duads) of the Signs. It concludes with 24 "Celebrity Snapshots", that reveal how their three key components and planetary aspects affect their appearance and personality.

Factors that can alter these primal "Zodiac Sign Features" are as follows:

(1) The **Sun**, **Moon** and **Ascendant** represent the functioning components in the human personality. All of these are rarely in the same Zodiac Signs.

(2) The **Aspects** between one's natal components and transiting planets color the nature of each of the Signs. As described on pages 4 and 5, they can combine, divide or redirect the nature of any involved components. This changes the dynamics and appearance of what we see in the Signs.

(3) The 17th century woodcut above shows the Zodiac Signs and the body parts that they rule. On the previous page, this book showed how each Zodiac Sign's **rulership of a different part of the body** dictates one's **body language**. These body mannerisms are described in greater detail in each of the following sections on each of the Signs.

(4) The **Houses** are the natural homes of the 12 Signs; As noted on page 18, they define the 12 arenas in our lives and the 4 quadrants in the chart—**where** we learn to (1) understand ourselves, (2) our environment, (3) our relationship to others—and (4) how we bring them all together into resolution.

The placement of a component in one of the Houses can color the manner in which its chart owner will approach that sector in his/her life. I.E., a Sun in Virgo's 6th House, often suggests he or she will find purpose in the field of health, or in jobs that require great attraction to detail.

Understanding these constantly changing forces can become overwhelming. Therefore, it is best that these astrological insights are only used as a tool—to help us understand ourselves, so that we can run with the flow of currents, that are far greater than our own.

Get Things Started *with your ARIES Friends!*

Aries
March 21 to April 19
(Dates vary slightly in some years)

Genesis: Masculine Polarity, Cardinal Fire

When the Sun journeys northward, over the equator on the dates above, it is the start of Spring in the northern hemisphere. Here, the stars of Aries are behind the Sun all month long. Also, everywhere around the world, at the break of dawn—the **Cardinal Fire** of **Aries** rises in the East.

On Earth's other half, the Sun's northward movement begins their season of Fall. Still, ALL individuals born in this month will show the traits of **Aries**, rather than **Libra**. This confirms that it is *the angle of Earth's Equatorial Plane to the Sun* that defines the character and physiognomy in all of the Sun Signs.

Fields of Likely Location:
The Ram charges forward, to explore new paths of discovery

Aries represents light's initial dominance over the night. Appropriately, it begins the **1st Quadran**t in the chart—and it rules the **1st House**, where one's journey of self discovery begins.

When the fiery spirit of the Aries Ram is ignited, they charge headfirst down the path, to explore their new found adventures. Individuals with an Aries Sun, Moon, or Rising Sign (or a strongly aspected Mars in a masculine sign) are likely to express the **Cardinal Fire** qualities of **Aries**.

To find one of these Rams, look in the hotter spots in your town, where *the action* is happening! Watch for those who are creating a lot of commotion, espousing their hardheaded opinions and brash ideas—as they debate the importance of individual expression. Of course, it will be their own opinions that they will consider to be the most important. Diplomats, they are not.

Aries Rams quickly grasp the essentials and aggressively make their points. They are the risk takers and the daring pioneers who begin new frontiers of discovery—for themselves and for those, who are their friends. In their more naive expressions, they become "The Children of the Zodiac".

To honor their unique gifts, give these fireballs unrestricted tasks. Let them be in charge—to initiate the actions, plow away the clutter and get things moving again. Be aware, if you tie them down, these creatures will quickly lose interest and pursue other adventures. All of us, who are left behind, will have to finish the job. Most of the physical work will be completed by the next Sign in the Zodiac: **Taurus**.

Associations and Rulerships: The Planet Mars

Appropriately, **Mars**, the God of War is the ruler of masculine Aries. The feminine version was traditionally assigned to be the ruler of **Scorpio**; Today, it is ruled by **Pluto**. This dwarf planet symbolizes the outer shell or edge of our solar "bio-system".

Mars is associated with the color "red", iron, diamonds, the military, all things of war, leaders in general, physical movement and athletic activity, the muscular and urogenital systems and the adrenal glands and energy carrying blood. It is also C. G. Jung's **Animus**, the masculine nature that operates in both sexes.

Careers often include fireman, engineers, butchers, metal workers and professional sportsman. This quest for self-identity begins in the 1st House.

Physical Traits ~ Aries rules the Head

As noted previously (page 30), all Signs rule a part of the body and this rulership changes the body's language and mannerisms. Since Aries rules the head, it is directed forward from the rest of the body—to lead the forward charge!

The large Aries head (and the convex bone structure in the face) resemble the physical traits of a Ram. The profile illustration shows how the Ram's prominent nose sweeps forward, and how the forehead and chin tilt to the back. This facial structure stretches the flesh around the nose. It also creates the muscular folds in the middle of the face and also the modeled plate on the forehead.

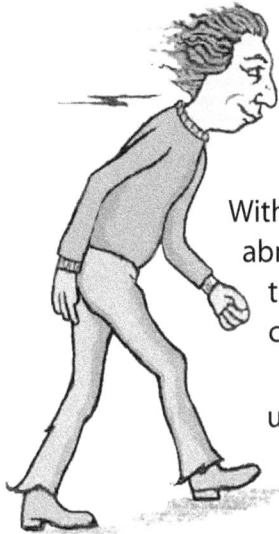

With the chin's sharp turn to the back, the tip of the nose abruptly narrows—and this forms indents just above each of the nostrils. On top of the Ram's head lies the reddish double-crowned tuffs of hair, that mock the shape of a sheep's horns.

Lucy Lawless, with her Aries Sun, Moon and Rising Sign, showed us the highly-directed mannerisms and powerful martial forces of Aries in her "*Warrior Princess*" role. With her Sun's ruling planet Mars in Taurus and Saturn on her Sun, Lucy is also remarkably sensual and grounded—for a triple Aries!

The Aries Suns above display varying degrees of the aggressive and forceful drive of **Cardinal Fire**. *Leonard Nimoy* and *William Shatner* are the true pioneers who have "taken us where no one has gone before". *Celine Dion* is the only triple fire in the group. *Eddie Murphy's* cardinality is anchored by his Fixed Leo Rising and Scorpio Moon. *James Franco* and *Hugh Hefner* show how strong water and Earth components douse the fire.

Meanwhile, *Lady GaGa*, *Reba McIntire* and *Sarah Jessica Parker* demonstrate us how their Gemini Ascendants stir and spread the fires. Surprisingly, *Alex Baldwin's* Moon is in Libra, but his Sun sextiles his Mars. (That explains his legendary short temper). The Cardinal force runs strong in all of these Aries—and that is why all of these people have gained recognition for initiating and succeeding in their own creative projects.

Determine Real Values, *with your TAURUS Friends!*

♉ Taurus
April 20 to May 20

Genesis and Classification:
Feminine Polarity, Fixed Earth

In midsummer, in the northern hemisphere, the hazy and lazy sunlight of **Taurus** shines throughout the day. This infuses a determination to support Aries' seedlings, so they can grow and give the Earth its greatest month of physical growth. All this "stuff" arouses the senses of the Taurus Bull!

South of the equator, it is Mid-Fall and the season of **Scorpio** is making resources scarcer. There, the Fixed Earth of Taurus rises everyday behind the morning Sun—to remind everyone that they need to get to work, to gather in the resources that will be needed, in the days ahead.

Taurus is the ruler of the **2nd House** in the chart. Individuals with Taurus Suns, Moons and Rising Signs (or a strongly aspected Venus in a feminine sign) will often express the qualities of Taurus.

Fields of Likely Location:
In green pastures, Bovines contentedly graze

You'll likely find your contented Taurus friends in quiet places, where Aries and the other Fire Signs seldom dwell. Look for lush environments, those filled with green, brown and earthy tones. Resting in the shadows, you will find these mellow bovines with their firm smiles and glazed eyes, grazing on delicious treats. Few words are needed to explain their sense of joy.

When the bovine eyes of Taurus focus on the content in their surroundings, they see all of the colorful and beautiful creations of Nature. Watch how their nostrils spread, when the nose gently touches a flower to capture its delightful aromas. Soon, you may see the contented smile, as their ears hear the music of the singing birds in the trees. In these delightful moments, these bovine creatures have little reason to move, until their senses inspire them to visit the greener pasture, that lies just down the road.

If you need to determine what has value and substance, call a Taurus friend. They know what things are worth! Let them be your banker and financial consultant, or better yet, put them to work building your home or any physical structure. They know how to get things done, for physical work is rarely shunned.

Negatively, these creatures can become extremely stubborn, self-indulgent, lazy and also obsessed with accumulating wealth. Some may withdraw into their lonely object-oriented worlds, alone with their often unused possessions. These inflexible tendencies are loosened, altered and expanded with the upcoming progression into the next Sign in the Zodiac: The **Mutable Air Sign** of **Gemini**.

♀ Associations and Rulerships: Ruling Planet ~ Venus

Venus' association with personal enjoyment and contentment is shown in its rulership of the feminine Sign of **Taurus**. Here, these Venusian senses are kept raw and simple, not arty or complex, as seen in the highly mental enhancements of Venus' co-rulership of **Libra**.

Venus' rulership of receptive Taurus represents C. G. Jung's **Anima**, the feminine Venusian desire that _attracts_ others to one's self. Venus' rulership of Masculine Libra is the **Animus**—the projected desire to gain the appeal of others. (See the Libra section on page 46) .

Taurus is associated with banks, buildings, land, real estate, treasures and possessions. Bovine's senses are attracted to stone sapphire stones, copper and the fragrances of Nature's flowers. Professions include farming, builders, architects and bankers. Since Taurus rules the throat, many Taurus souls are singers.

Physical Traits ~ Taurus rules the Throat, Neck and Shoulders

The rulership of body areas progresses downward in the same order as the Zodiac Signs. From **Aries'** rulership of the head, the energies shift down into the neck and shoulders—the region of the body ruled by **Taurus**. Unlike the head-butting charge of the Ram, the placement of these internalized feminine energies (in this part of the body) restricts any forward movement. Note how the forward lean of the shoulders pushes the lower torso to the back. This weight bows the legs, as it plants the feet firmly in the ground.

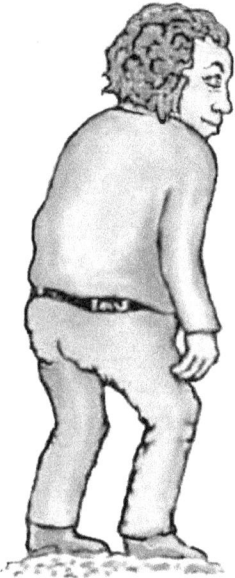

This body rulership (and the fixed modality of Earth) defines this creature's physical features. Most notable are the heavy shoulders, the massive bones and torso, and the stocky arms and legs. Notably, *Robert Pattinson* and *Gigi Hadi* both have Taurus Suns and Ascendants.

Gigi's 5º Ascendant is in the "Taurus decan" or first ten-degrees of Taurus. Since the Ascendant affects the bone structure, her facial features and skull reflect the square qualities of Taurus. Meanwhile, Robert has a 14º Virgo decan Ascendant. This makes his face longer and slightly skewed. (*See Decans on page 72*).

Both of these folks share Taurus' most obvious feature —the fully pupilled and fixed bovine eyes. Note how they rise up on the outer edges, when they focus onto the physical delights in their surroundings.

These Taurus Sun Signs show how other components alter the appearance of **Fixed Earth**. *George Lucas* shows the staid and anchored persona of his Taurus Ascendant. *Cate Blanchett* (also a Taurus Rising) shows how the bovine eyes form, when she projects the light of their Taurus Sun. *Daniel Day Lewis* shows how the mellowness disappears, when his Capricorn Ascendant rises, to turn the Earth into granite.

Even with their Water Ascendants, *Cher* (before cosmetic adjustments), *George Clooney* and *Adele* still display Taurus' highly recognized eyes. In contrast, *Michelle Pfieffer* and *Dwayne Johnson* often show the lightness of their airy Gemini and Libra Ascendants. Meanwhile, *Jack Nicholson* and *Barbra Steisand* display the sizzle of their fiery Leo and Aries Ascendants.

Think of the Possibilities, with your GEMINI Friends!

Ⅱ Gemini
May 21 to June 20
Genesis and Classification:
Masculine Polarity, Mutable Air

In the last month of every season, it's time to break from the holding pattern of Fixity. This task is the job of the Zodiac's Mutable Signs, who make the changes that will prepare us for the new season that lies ahead.

It is the end of **Spring** in the northern hemisphere, and all around the world on the dates above, the Sign of **Gemini** is rising behind the morning Sun. Every morning, life is stirred—as it is awakened by the force of **Mutable Air**.

Geminis are the students who analyze the contents in our surroundings and then put them into the words, that will communicate their learned insights to others. This desire to learn is also seen in people, who have a Sun, Moon and Ascendant in Gemini—or strong aspects to their Mercury.

Fields of Likely Location:
In twisting gusts of air, the Twins bring new ideas into form

When the breezes of Gemini are activated, one spiral of Air spins clockwise, while the other swirls in the opposite direction. You'll see this in the hands of Geminis, when they express their ideas to others. The resulting electricity of this exchange sparks the minds of everyone in the room.

Look in open air places, filled with chatter and conversation. If you see a person fluttering around the room, engaging conversions with everyone, it is likely he or she is a Gemini. That person and the other Geminis in the room, will be wearing colorful clothing—with lighter shades of blue and smatterings of yellow or orange. Many, like *Cindi Lauper* and *Prince* will often display an outrageous mix of tie-dyed colors.

It is said that the best way to keep youthful, is to keep the mind active and curious. So, get up out of your soft Venusian couch—and start a conversation with a Gemini friend! In just a few minutes, your mind will be buzzing with new ideas. They will likely inspire you to make some exciting changes in your life.

In negative expression, the Gemini twins run in countering directions, splitting everything into dueling infinities. These scattered thoughts can break down any chain of logic and make further analysis impossible. To give these wayward ideas purpose and direction, they need to be guided by the personal feelings and emotions, that are initiated by the next Sign in the Zodiac: **Cancer.**

Associations and Rulerships: Ruling Planet ~ Mercury

Mercury regulates our minds, nervous systems and thinking process. In masculine **Gemini**, Mercury suggests the act of *inductive reasoning*, where multiple pieces are combined together, to form larger concepts. In Mercury's co-rulership of feminine **Virgo**, the *deductive* mind does the opposite—as it breaks these complex arrangements into singular units of thought.

Gemini's rulership of the **3rd House of Communication** tells the nature of the words (and the field of study) that a student will pursue in his/her life. This journey begins with the dialogue they have with their immediate family, namely those of their siblings. The curiosity is soon expanded with short trips to places, near their Cancerian homes. These trips are often taken on bicycles, scooters and small vehicles.

Careers for Gemini include journalism, broadcasting, teaching, writing and anything that has to do with words. They are often travel agents, chauffeurs and postal workers.

40

Physical Traits ~ Gemini rules the lungs, arms and hands

Moving downward from **Taurus'** neck and shoulders—the force of life is now is placed in the arms, hands and lungs—the area of the body ruled by **Gemini**. Here, the dueling force of mutability regulates the in-and-out breathing in the two lungs, as it pins the arms and hands in two directions.

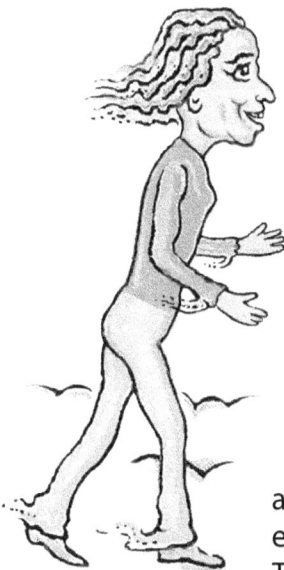

When Geminis fly down their paths, their twirling hands (like propellers on a plane) drive them forward. As the head turns from left to right, it acts like a rudder on a plane. Any change-in-thought changes the course of flight. These aerated energies give these aeronauts their lanky arms and legs and thin torsos.

With a Gemini Ascendant to enhance the traits of their chatty Suns, *Gene Wilder* and *Dr. Ruth Westheimer* both display the skewed features, the two broad front teeth, the sparkling, offset eyes—and the long, thin-bridged nose that dips abruptly at the tip.

Gene and Ruth show how Gemini's parallel cheeks run forward from the upper half of the face. This forms the rectangular jaw and chin assembly. This shape is also clearly displayed in the *Angelina Jolie* and *Bob Dylan* images below.

Note how their billowing flesh duplicates the lines and features in the face. They appear to have two eyelids and two sets of lips. In other words: There are two faces, where only one should be.

With *Angelina Jolie*, *Tim Allen* and *Anderson Cooper*, the swirling currents of **Mutable Air** are highly driven by their Aries Moons. *Cooper's* presence is calmer and so is *Annette Bening*—for they have Libra Ascendants. *Joan Rivers'* Aries Rising and Sag Moon make her the true chatterbox in this group. *Paul McCartney* and *Clint Eastwood* have Leo Moons. *Bob Dylan* rounds out the Fire list with his Centaur Ascendant, but he often appears surprisingly grounded. He has Five components (including his Taurus Moon) in Earth Signs.

Others with strong receptive components include *Clint Eastwood* and *Nicole Kidman*, who both have Scorpio Risings. This accounts for his "Dirty Harry" persona and her "seductive" presence.

Marilyn Monroe, with three water planets and heavy Neptune aspects, shows the difficulties that can occur, when one's emotions are constantly churned by the Mutable Force of Air.

♋ Cancer
June 21 to July 22

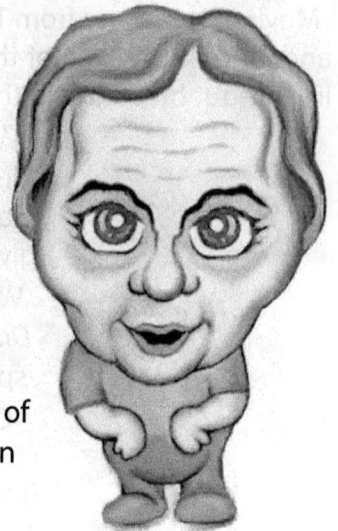

Genesis: Feminine Polarity, Cardinal Water

On the Solstices, the Sun reaches its highest point in the northern hemisphere and it lowest in the southern half. On both ends, the Sun reverses direction, to begin its movement back to the equator. Throughout this month, the Sign of Cancer rises behind the morning Sun, all around the world,

With this polar shift and redirection, all souls are directed—to secure a place of shelter in their unstable and stormy environment. This drive is more obvious in Cancer Crabs, since they are emotionally pulled and pushed by the constant Cardinal shifts in direction—in the Earth's daily lunar tides.

With their awareness of the lunar cycles, Cancers not only feel the directional changes in the currents, they also sense the shift of cadence that is occurring in Nature's repetitive cycles. This constant ebb and flow in the crab's surroundings instills a strong desire to find a place to rest—and call home!

With the Moon's rulership of Cancer, the round "lunar temples" dominate the face. This feature is strong in most Cancer Ascendants, and also in other Sun Signs who have Cancer Moons.

Fields of Likely Location:
In tidal pools, the Crab finds shelter from the storm

Settled in the comfort of their homes, these children of the Moon calmly wait for the special moment—when another tidal wave rolls past their front door! With anticipation, they'll slide into the stream, then surf the crest of the wave, to the nearby places—where they will find needed treasures for their families.

When the tide shifts—they'll ride the wave back home, with their arms filled with valued booty. Strangely, even with their closets filled to the brim, these creatures are always ready to make another "gathering run".

Look in damp and secluded places, where waters quietly run. There, you'll find the happy crab, cooking soup to nourish others. **Aries** is way down the road. **Gemini** is on the telephone. **Taurus** is drawn to the aromas of the bubbling stew. The crab kindly serves another bowl. That's why Cancers and Tauruses get along!

When these creatures lose their sense of direction, they become insecure, emotional and incredibly crappy. Some will withdraw into their shells and separate themselves from any contact with others. However, those who become comfortable in 'their space", will soon acquire the sense of confidence, that will allow them to step out into the world—and express their feelings to others! This occurs, when the Sun enters **Leo**.

Associations and Rulerships: The Moon is the ruler of Cancer

One's home is found in the 4th House in the chart. This House and the Sign of Cancer are ruled by the Moon—the Goddess of our instincts, our habits and emotional reactions. These lunar tides regulate the sympathetic nervous system, body fluids and the memory. The Sign of Cancer is associated with menstrual cycles, the diaphragm, the breasts, the womb, the esophagus and the fluids that enable the swallowing of nutritious food.

Cardinal Water is the mothering force, that drives individuals to create and sustain a family home—and the memory of bygone ancestors. Cancer's rulership of the upper digestive system is why cooking, food and most kitchen utensils are associated with this Sign.

The crab's metal is silver and her stone is the ocean's pearl. These Moon children are attracted to flowering plants and trees rich in sap. Cancers are excellent as business persons, caring nurses, boat-builders, caterers, housewives, kindergarten teachers, antique dealers and museum curators.

Physical Traits ~ Cancer rules the breasts and the upper torso

When body rulership progresses downward into the breasts and upper torso, the energies are centered in the largest part of the body. Here, the tides of Cancer *pull the chest down and to the front*. This throws the shoulders and neck to the back. These crabs have to look upwards, to see what is right in front of them.

The gangly arms and craws of these Crabs are pulled in tightly to the body, to anchor them securely into their space of occupancy. Any movement out of this comfort zone begins when the crab takes a step forward. With the placement of one foot forward, the heavy shell is thrown off balance in the direction of that leading foot. The crab has to shuffle sideways, to shift the weight back to the other side. Once in a upright position, the next step throws the torso in the opposite direction. This starts the process again.

The *Dali Lama* and *Liv Tyler* have Cancer Ascendants and Suns. This accentuates their "shell-shaped" crab faces. Note how their thin bridged noses mark the center of the circle formed by their round temples.

On the forehead, wavy lines appear to mock the lines on the back of a crab's shell. Below, their often small mouths are placed just above their short, round chins.

The rapid changing Moon accounts for the crab's shifting emotions, and also the regular swelling and receding that we see in their facial features.

Here, as the currents of **Cardinal Water** wax and wane, the faces of these crabs rearrange into a variety of liquid expressions. Cancer's presence is proudly presented in the Leo Rising faces of *Anthony Bourdan*, *Jane Lynch* and *Meryl Streep*. The Centaur Ascendants of *Princess Diana* and *Nelson Mandala* add a fiery spark to their personalities. *Benedict Cumberbatch's* Libra Rising makes him a remarkably cerebral crab.

All of the four folks on the right have prominent water components. *Will Ferrell's* Scorpio Moon is filtered thru his Virgo Ascendent; This makes him mercuric and controlling. *Robin Williams* and *Debra Harry* have Scorpio Rising and Pisces Moons; The mutable patterns are obvious in their faces. *Arianna Huffington* also has Scorpio Rising, but *her Moon is in Cancer*. With the Moon being the ruler of her Sun and Moon, her face swells and brightly beams—more so than all the others!

43

♌ Leo July 23 to August 22

Genesis & Class: Masculine Polarity, Fixed Fire

In the middle of Spring, **Taurus** aroused our senses with Earth's physical delights. Here, it is Midsummer in the northern hemisphere and Mid-Fall in the other half. In both halves, the Sign of Leo is parked behind the Sun. All month long, the fabulous glow of Fixed Fire's Light appears at sunrise, all around the world. This inspires individuals to fulfill their personal creative desires—and make their Cancer neighborhoods a delightful place to play!

Watch how these kings and queens confidently step onto the stage—to announce their grandiose visions on how to dress up our drab and lackluster neighborhoods. They may want to construct a playground in the park, build a theater to entertain the citizens or create the most elegant restaurant in town.

This spark of Fixed Fire is not just in the hearts of Leos—it's in all of us! But with our different Suns, our creative visions are cast in differently colored lights. Those who have a Leo Sun, Moon or Rising Sign will likely have visions, that are far more grandiose than the rest of us.

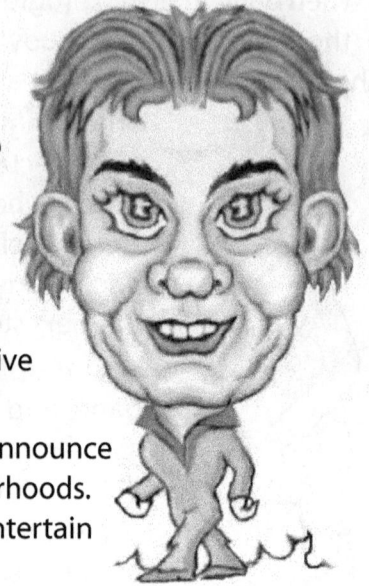

Fields of Likely Location:
In the spotlight, the Lion proudly creates playful visions

Visit the classy and elegant spots in your town, where beautiful people play. If you hear boisterous and confident voices, unflappably upstaging each other—you have encountered a pride of Lions.

Watch how the Fixed Fires of Leo glow, when these lions attract the attention of others. That desire to be in the spotlight is instantaneous and conceived in the moment. Many will follow, for Leo knows what has to be done—in this moment of time—to make our neighborhoods and communities better! Meanwhile, on the other side of the Zodiac, **Aquarius** is focused on forecasting future trends and projects.

So join in, for your time with these lions will be fondly remembered as being very exciting—but just remember, some of your contributions may be quickly forgotten—for many of these self-centered lions will want to take all of the credit—for they firmly believe that they "created everything!"

Positively, these grandiose Lion concepts inspire all of us to "go to work", so that we can make our neighborhoods and communities a delightful place for our children to play. [Leo also symbolizes the father.]

To get it all done, the grounded and mutable forces in the next Sign of **Virgo** are needed, to bring the changes that will make Leo's inspired vision a reality. It'll take a lot of hard work; Without it—nothing works.

Associations and Rulerships: The Sun is the ruler of LEO

The Fixed Fire of Leo is ruled by the Sun, since the Sun is fixed in the center of our solar system. Perhaps, that is why so many Leos think that everything evolves around them?
Leos are often surrounded by the colors of yellow, red and Orange. (Royal Purple is also popular, but the first 3 colors are what we see in the coat of a Lion). Appropriately, Leo's metal is Gold and the Ruby is their stone. Oranges, flowers, rosemary and all citrus trees compliment their energies.

Careers include all things in the field of entertainment: Actors, dancers, directors, and any position involving promotion and publicity. Leos also are skilled managers of people, youth workers and wonderful teachers, since they can inspire others to be creative. Some make excellent astrologers.

Physical Traits ~ Leo rules the heart, the back and the spine

It is the heart, that pumps blood throughout the body. This fire-red liquid supplies the oxygen of **Gemini** and the nourishments of **Cancer**—to feed and empower the spark of life, that runs through the spine. The heart, back and spine are all under the rulership of the Sign of **Leo**.

With their hearts leading them forward, these lions "stand tall", as they strut onto the stage. Watch how their barrel-like chests expand to the front. This often occurs, when these cats recognize that they are drawing attention from others. With this adulation, the glowing coals in Leo's internal furnace, quickly erupt into a burst of theatrical flares.

To begin this examination of Leo's physical traits, we have two pureblood Lions: *Garrison Keillor* and *Rose Marie*. Both have Leo Suns and Rising Signs. *Garrison*, in his radio show "Prairie Home Companion" told us of his hometown, where every child was above average. Rose's theatrical antics lit up "The Dick Van Dyke Show".

Note how most of these folk's bone structure and facial expressions mock the features of a Lion. This is supported by the cubical forehead with its burly mane, huge protruding ears and the bushy fixed brow. Below, their feline eyes are firmly set above the wide-bridged and square tipped nose. Most of these Leos show fixity's cubical features, the stubby, wide-based nose, the high and wide-set cheekbones, the wide-set nostrils, the rectangular jaw and the square chin of the lion.

Most of these Leos show fixity's cubical features—i.e., the stubby, wide-based nose, the high and wide-set cheekbones and the rectangular jaw of the lion. *Andy Warhol's* Leo Rising makes him a bodacious lion! With his Fixed Scorpio Ascendant and Moon, movie director *Stanley Kubrick* appears far more intense, while *Jerry Garcia* (with his Libra Ascendant) appears as "laid-back" as his music. *Mick Jagger* and *Jennifer Lawrence* (with their Gemini and Sagittarius Ascendants) are the most animated of the bunch, while *Jackie Kennedy* and *Robert DeNiro*'s water Ascendants douse the fire. With the Earth of Taurus Rising, *Halle Berry*, *Melanie Griffith* and *Delta Burke* appear to be the most anchored of the group.

It's time to work things out—and bring the plan to completion

Virgo

August 23 to September 22

Genesis: Feminine Polarity, Mutable Earth

Once again, it is the end of a season and a Mutable Sign takes control. On both halves of the Globe, the Sun is in the Sign of Virgo—and on all locations around the Earth, Virgo rises at the break of dawn.

This force of Mutable Earth inspires (and enables) individuals to perform the work and services, that will prepare the Earth for new season ahead.

Our Virgo friends are acutely awareness of the littlest details. With their mercuric and deductive minds, they are highly capable of breaking down complex arrangements into their tiniest of parts—and then reassemble them into more functional wholes. With this, *they can make the visions of Leo a reality!*

Individuals with a Virgo Sun, Moon, or Rising Sign—or a strongly aspected Mercury (in a feminine sign) will often express the perfectionism of Mutable Earth.

Fields of Likely Location:
Amidst the clutter, Virgo creates physical order

Check out the headquarters of any major organization or business. Look for the room where shelves are filled with books, research material and engineering plans. Next, find the desk with the biggest piles of papers. Likely a Virgo will be perched in the chair, busily reorganizing the stuff into neater arrangements.

With the force of Mutable Earth at their disposal, Virgos have an incredible ability to sort through hundreds of details and then rearrange them into workable plans. With these plans, their **Taurus** partners can construct the structures, envisioned by **Leo**. The person, directing the whole operation, will likely be the third Earth Sign: **Capricorn**.

In the midst of any project, Virgo's eyebrows alternately shift up and down, as they search for undiscovered details. Watch how, when they find a needed bit of information, their eyes flicker with electricity. The sparkling lights tell you that Mercury's Messenger has arrived—to present the ideas, and then plant them into Virgo's mercuric mind.

Virgo's obsession with insignificant details gives some of these souls a limited breadth of vision. This can lead to nervousness, criticalness, excessive worrying and hypochondria. They are brought into balance and given creative direction—by the Cardinal Air of the next Sign in the Zodiac: **Libra**.

Associations and Rulerships: Ruling Planet ~ Mercury

They cycles of the planet Mercury regulate the analytical, reasoning and logistical process within the act of thinking. **Virgo** is associated with *deductive thinking*, the act of finding the smaller pieces in a larger whole. Virgo's specific-oriented observations are balanced by the broader generalizations and *inductive reasonings* of masculine **Gemini**, the other Sign ruled by the planet of Mercury. With **Mutable Earth**, analytical endeavors are performed—to serve the physical needs of others. All things associated with health, service and daily routines to promote cleanliness are placed in the **6th House**, the House ruled by Virgo.

Good careers for these servants include scientists, statisticians, gardeners, accountants, teachers, and any job that deals with health and hygiene.

Physical Traits: Virgo rules the stomach & upper digestive track

From Leo's **Heart**, body rulership slides down into the **upper digestive track** and **stomach**—the body part ruled by the Sign of **Virgo**. This, and the switch to passive Earth, greatly alters the body language.

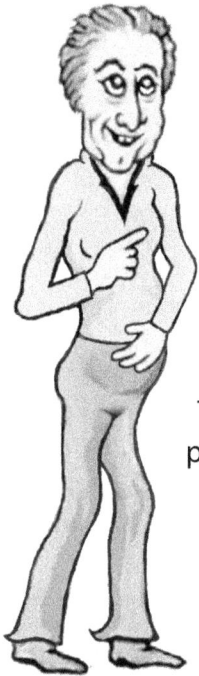

Placement in the body's midsection pushes the chest and shoulders to the back, as it lifts the buttocks upward. This creates a protruding upper stomach.

This gives these people a stilted walk, that (with every step) sways the stomach left to right. Unlike the expansive Air of Mercury-ruled **Gemini**, the hands of receptive **Virgo** remain close to the body, shielding the body's "virginal parts".

Keannu Reeves and *Peter Sellers* are examples of Virgos, who also have Virgo rising. Reeves shows the high forehead, the squinted offset eyes and how the pointed nose and chin shoot off in opposite directions. Sellers shows a more rugged face, with his chunky and jowly features. Note how their upper skulls (and most of those below) bulge off to the left—or to the right at the top.

To demonstrate the strength of the Ascendant, a photo of **Leo** *Madonna* is included. She has **Virgo Rising** and therefore, her bone structure gives her the long neck and the wide gap between her front teeth. (The gap is similar to what we see in Seller's frontal teeth). This Lioness may be showy, but she looks "just like a Virgin".

The faces of the above Virgo Sun Signs are torqued and twisted by the Mutable forces. More than any other Mutable Sign, Virgo's skewed features are the easiest to detect, since they're anchored in the solid clay of the Element of Earth. *Richard Gere, Dr. Phil McGraw* and *Sean Connery* display Virgo's offset cheekbones, twisted noses and angled chins. *Lauren Bacall, Cameron Diaz, Leanne Rimes* and *Amy Poehler* show how Virgo's asymmetrical eyes and facial features can be so beautiful. Meanwhile, *Oliver Stone* reveals the common gap in Virgo's upper center teeth, while *Lily Tomlin* and *Paul Reubins* (aka, Pee Wee Herman) demonstrate what happens, when the mercuric and nervous energies of Virgo run amuck.

Maintain the Balance *with your LIBRA Friends!*

♎ Libra
Masculine Polarity, Cardinal Air
September 23 to October 22

On September 23, the **Sun** moves CCW into the 3rd Quadrant and upper half of the chart. Here, the equator's angle to the Sun brings **Fall's Solstice** to the northern hemisphere, and Spring to the lower half of the globe. All month long, the Sun is in **Libra**—and on every place on Earth, the Sun rises every day, with the Sign of *Libra behind the morning Sun*. All who are born in this month will display the traits of **Cardinal Air**, and the Venusian qualities of **Libra.**

Six months ago, the Sign of **Aries** rose over the eastern equator, to bring the season of Spring to the northern hemisphere. There, the dominant light began the Ram's journey of self-discovery. Now, with **Libra** behind the Sun, *this movement into the other half* activates the **Cardinal Air** of Libra—to direct our thoughts to less personal activities.

Here, the Venusian materials of **Taurus** are weighted and evaluated—to determine their physical worth, function and esthetic value. With Libra's view of the other side, we can now share the resources with others—and make our planet a lovelier place to be!

Fields of Likely Location:
When opposing fronts collide, Libra calms the storm.

The 1st Law of Thermodynamics suggests that all dominate forces will eventually dissipate and then reform into evenly balanced arrangements. Energy is not lost, it is just redistributed and turned into other forms. Cardinal Air represents this act of bringing everything into balance—to create more creative arrangements!

Looking to bring balance into your life? Check out the more pleasant locations in your town—perhaps the library, a pastry shop, or any place with pastel-colored walls, beautiful paintings and artful arrangements of fine furniture. If you hear a group quietly discussing the arts, justice and interpersonal relationships—and the conversation is even-toned, without a hint of argument—then you've likely found a group of Libras.

This gathering welcomes all cultures and ideas that support justice and equality. Many often take the position of the underdog—but they'll also quickly switch sides—when the underdog achieves dominant status. For Libras, consensus is never easy, for this world is filled with a diversity of individuals, each with their own acquired opinions. This makes it difficult for many Libras to "take a side".

To counter these indecisive tendencies, **Scorpio**—the next Sign in the Zodiac—provides the emotional focus, that will help them to define the actions, that will be needed—to solve what appears to be a seemingly insolvable resolution.

Associations and Rulerships: Ruling Planet ~ Venus

Venus' association with personal enjoyment was introduced in the Feminine Sign of **Taurus.** In the Masculine Sign of **Libra**, these Venusian forces are expanded to refine the finer pleasures of the senses, through the use of ideas and artful expressions. This suggests why Libra rules the kidneys, the organ that refines and purifies needed materials for the body.

Persons with a strongly aspected Venus in a Masculine Sign, often express the qualities of Cardinal Air. Here, they are projecting C. G. Jung's **Anima** outward—*to make themselves attractive to others!* This Sign's colors are pale blue and pink, the colors that are often seen in Opal, Libra's birthstone.

Libra's gift for forming agreements accounts for their careers as professional consultants, lawyers, and judges. Venus' association with romance and knowledge is seen in the careers of <u>Libra</u>rians, welfare workers, beauticians, fashion designers, and in any of the fields of the finer arts.

Physical Traits Libra rules the kidneys, lumbar region, & the skin's surface

The rulership of areas in the body started at the head, in **Aries**. Appropriately, when we reach the midpoint between the head and the **Pisces**-ruled feet, we are in the body region ruled by the opposite Sign of Aries—**Libra**.

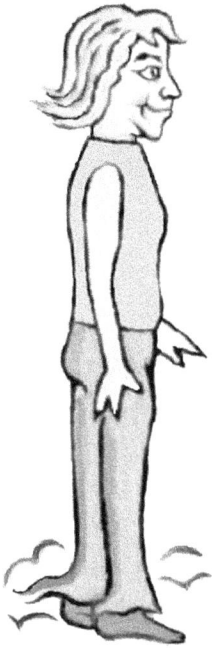

Here, the lumbar and kidneys make up most of this area of the body, but traditionally, Libra also rules the surface of the skin. These rulerships account for Libra's perfectly proportioned features, their creamy smooth skin and their easy-going, well-balanced mannerisms. Appropriately, sections of their bodies are evenly proportioned and the body is full and rounded like a cumulus cloud—smooth and fluffy, but rarely light and thin.

When Libras glide across the floor, their bodies appear perfectly erect. Their hands are held low, with fingers pointing to the sides. The torso teeters left and right, to maintain the balance, as the arms float low on the sides. If one arm moves outward, the other counters in an equal distance. Some seem to walk like they have a book balanced on their heads.

Barbara Walters and *Jimmy Carter* are both Libras with Libra rising. In their bone structure and facial features, the shapes and qualities of Libra are enhanced, since the solar expressions and *the mask* are one and the same. Since there is no filter to slow their delivery of words, these two always expressed "what they were thinking"—without any hesitation!

These Libra Sun Signs exhibit varying degrees of the equalizing force and drive of **Cardinal Air**. *Will Smith* and *Sigourney Weaver* both project the sideways push of Cardinal Air. *Cheryl Tiegs, Gwynth Paltrow* and *Kamala Harris,* with their ever present smiles, present the natural beauty of Venus' influence.

John Lennon and *Dwight "Ike" Eisenhower* showed their power of persuasion, in peace and war. *President Ike, Mickey Mantle, Kelly Ripa* and *Matt Damon* strongly display Libra's most recognizable facial features—the level eyebrows, thin eyelids and the sparkling almond eyes that stretch out to the sides.

In all images, you'll notice how the spherical cheekbones cap their widespread V-shaped smiles. This smile runs from ear to ear, to form the long vertical dimples on the side of the cheeks.

Hold on to what is meaningful, *with your SCORPIO Friends!*

Scorpio
October 23 to November 21
Genesis: Feminine Polarity, Fixed Water

In the Season of Mid-Fall, the days are getting colder and resources are becoming scarce. With these disturbing events, there is an emotional need to review the evaluations of **Libra** and determine the true value of our current resources. With these insights—we can determine the martial actions, that we will need to take—to prepare for the long winter ahead!

With the **Fixed Water** of **Scorpio** rising in the morning light, people around the world are emotionally resolved, to hold on to all resources of value—and discard all things of little worth. With these actions, individuals gain their personal sense of power—and the emotional strength—to sustain themselves, not only thru the coming winter, but also for the many years, that lie ahead.

If you feel uncertainty in your life, call a Scorpio friend. They'll show you how to *get your emotions under control* and find the strength, to "make it thru the night". Individuals with an Scorpio Sun, Moon or Rising Sign (or a strongly aspected Pluto or Mars in a feminine Sign) often express the qualities of Fixed Water. The empowerment comes from the Scorpion, and it is the Eagle's wings that lift us out of the darkness.

In the shadows between dark and light, Scorpio hides the magical secrets

These Fixed Water souls can be found in places, where powerful people gather. If you walk in confidently as you pass thru the heavy iron door, others with think you belong there, and no one will stop you. Once inside, you'll see that the walls are dark (usually ruby red with black trim), and the room is filled with heavy furniture and ornately-framed pictures of powerful bygone leaders. You have entered a den of scorpions! Instantly, you'll notice there's little arguing, for the conversations seem to be "merged together" in collective consensus. These folks know each other's secrets and they know who's feeding them a line of crap.

This knowing is empowering, but it also has its "darker side". Some will use their secrets to manipulate others. And there are those, who refuse to share their insights, for fear of losing control. Positively, many Scorpions know that true power comes from their emotional attachments with others. With this bond, there is no fear. With their empowered wings, these Eagles lift themselves up from the ashes, to soar upward into the heavens above! This freeing of the spirit comes from the next Sign in the Zodiac: **Sagittarius**.

Associations and Rulerships: Ruling Planet ~ Pluto (traditionally Mars)

On page 28, this book noted that Venus and Mars are the ruling planets of two Signs—one for a Feminine Sign and the other for a Masculine Sign. As noted, **Taurus** and **Libra** are ruled by **Venus**. In earlier days, **Aries** and **Scorpio** were ruled by **Mars**. Today, the outer planet of **Pluto** became the **ruler** of **Scorpio**. In classical mythology, Pluto was the name given to the Underworld of Hades. Pluto's placement in the chart enables astrologers to interpret the longer cycles in one's life—as well as those that occur in the passing of generations!

With the long-range cycles of Pluto, the mysteries of the regenerative and transforming processes in life are revealed. Pluto lies on the "outer eggshell of our solar system". This suggests the totality of Nature's bionic experiences: Sex, reproduction, birth, death and the afterlife. Amazingly, Pluto's 248 year orbit supports the ancient adage that **"All of your actions affect Seven Generations"**. *[7 generations at 35 years each = 245 years].*

Scorpio is also associated with hypnosis, hidden and secret underworld forces and catastrophic transformations (eruptions and earthquakes). Careers for Scorpios include police, detectives, the military, psychics, psychologists and spiritual healers. Many of the world's best surgeons are Scorpios.

50

Physical Traits: Scorpio rules the pelvic region & reproductive organs

From the body's center point (**Libra**), rulership progresses down to the lower midsection, or the power base of the body. Here, the power of Fixed Water is concentrated in the pelvic area.

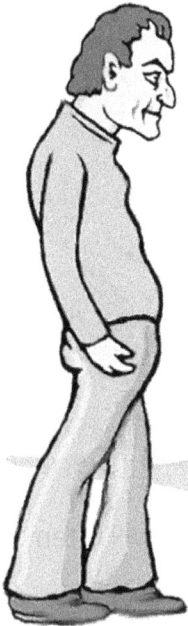

The resulting body stance draws the hips and pelvic region forward, as it sends the upper torso and the lower legs to the back. At the upper back, the neck and head jut sharply to the front—to create the recognizable "Eagle" profile! Note how the heavy, cupped arms hang to the sides, until the magic moment, when this bird takes off in flight.

Like the head of an eagle, the flat back section of Scorpio's skull tilts sharply forward, while the forehead angles to the back. The makes the head unusually narrow at the top. Note how the back of the skull runs in line, with the angle of the upper back.

To illustrate the phenomenon of the Scorpio profile, we have pictures of three Scorpio Suns: *Billy Graham, Neil Young* and *Grace Kelly* (who also has a Scorpio Ascendant). *Billy* and *Grace* show the sharp forward tilt in the upper back. *Neil* demonstrates how this forward tilt of the back skull, and the back-angled forehead narrows the top of the skull.

The focused emotional power of **Fixed Water** runs strong in these Scorpio Sun Signs. *Leo DiCaprio, Anne Hatcher* and *Matthew McConaughey* show how their powerful eyes fix onto distant prey, just before they attack. Scorpio's power of concentration is seen in *Adam Driver, Murray Abraham* and *Whoppi Goldberg*. *K.D. Lang* and *Emma Stone* show how their Eagle's eyes sweep up on the sides, just before they take off in flight. *Joaquin Phoenix* and *Jodi Foster* display the large pupillage and deeply intense eyes of Fixed Water.

Most of these individuals show the cubical skull, and the how fixed eyebrows rise on the outer edges. They also reveal the Eagle's prominent beak—and the flat and down-drawn cheek bones of Scorpio.

Aim for the impossible, *with your SAGITTARIUS Friends!*

Sagittarius
November 22 to December 21
Masculine Polarity, Mutable Fire

When the Sun enters the last month in the year, many individuals are inspired to review the lessons that were initiated six months ago in **Gemini**, enhanced in the Autumn light of **Libra** and then empowered and defined by the deep insights of **Scorpio.** Now, at the end of the season of Fall, the expansive and Mutable Fires of Sagittarius are inspiring individuals to pursue higher levels of understanding. With this, we can make our resolutions for the New Year ahead.

With these resolutions and our life-time of acquired knowledge, we now understand the lessons that Nature has mastered, and wisely use her bounty, so that we can make it thru the coming Winter nights. That is why we have a day in this month to *give thanks* for what we have received.

Individuals with a Sagittarius Sun, Moon and/or Rising Sign (or a strongly aspected Jupiter) will often express the unrestrained qualities of Mutable Fire.

Fields of Likely Location:
The Centaur gallops away, to pursue higher knowledge

From the depths of our subconscious feelings, Scorpio has revealed the hidden truths. Now, as the *Mutable Fire* spreads in all directions, the *Phoenix* is freed, *to rise up from the ashes!* With this opening of the gates, all of us are free to join these fillies and stallions—as they gallop across the plains, kayak the meandering rivers and climb distant mountain peaks. The sense of joy is incredible!

In the more lively spots in town, these creatures are easy to spot. They may be the comedian on the stage, the hyena chuckling at the bar, or the DJ spinning the records after the comedian has completed his/her show. At any sporting event, these athletic Archers will likely be the ones playing on the field.

You'll likely find these ponies in big, open spaces—in parks or in large, open-windowed facilities. The conversations will be feisty, complex and far more philosophical than the analytic dialogue that we witnessed with **Gemini.** This sense of non-attachment runs strong with Sagittariuses. For some, the fires spread out of control, as they become blindly optimistic, wasteful and over indulgent. These scattered energies are contained and given direction by the next Sign in the Zodiac: **Capricorn.**

Associations and Rulerships: Ruling Planet ~ Jupiter

Jupiter is the largest planet in the solar system. It's a big ball of gas! Appropriately, it symbolizes and rules the Sign of **Sagittarius**. In earlier days, it was also the ruler of feminine **Pisces**. Jupiter is known as "The Greater Benefic", who expands and opens the door of opportunity to all.

Opportunities often appear when planets transit the **9th House**. There, one is stirred to pursue knowledge, a new philosophy, higher education and/or speculative thinking. This expansive outlook often leads to long distance travel, the learning of other languages and the publishing of one's ideas to others.

For the Romans, *Jove* was the name for Jupiter. For the Greeks, the deity *Zeus* represented this planet. Jupiter's "12 year cycle of fortune" is associated with the 12 animals in the Chinese Zodiac.

Careers for Sagittarius include teachers, lecturers, lawyers, interpreters, veterinary surgeons, horse trainers, travel agents, sportsmen, priests, writers and any work that doesn't reign in this creature's roaming spirit.

Physical Traits: Sagittarius rules the thighs

When the body forces shift into the thighs, the energy is divided—as one high-stepping thigh propels these Centaurs in one direction—and the next step sends them in the opposite direction! As in the opposite Sign of **Gemini**, any change in attitude abruptly alters the course.

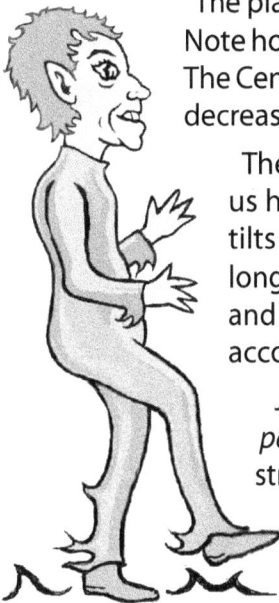

The placement of force in the thighs defines the Centaur's body language and appearance. Note how their chests and shoulders are abnormally flat in depth—and vertically stretched! The Centaur's body mass is concentrated in the pear-shaped hips and large thighs. This mass decreases from the knees downward, and in the lower parts ruled by the last three Signs.

The illustrations shows the half horse/half human features of the Centaur. It also gives us hints on this creature's body language, as it shows how the upper half of the body tilts to the back. The high-domed and back-swept foreheads, off-set eyes, angled jaw and long necks are seen in the photos of *Scarlett Johansson* and *Jake Gylenthaal*. Scarlett's Centaur rising accounts for her wide-toothed horse laugh.

Jakes' Leo Rising is in the Sag decan. *(See page 72)*. This alters the underlying skeletal structure to give him the long jaw of a horse, rather than the square one of a lion.

These traits are also seen in the Centaur Sun Signs below.

All of these Sagittarius Sun Signs exhibit the energy of **Mutable Fire**. *Dick Van Dyke* and *Ben Stiller* show the Centaur's gift for comedy. *Billie Elish, Christina Aquilara* and *Taylor Swift* all have "music creating" Neptune aspecting one of their luminaries; Notably, Swift's 6 Neptune aspects make her a prolific composer.

Along with *Brad Pitt*, Swift also has 5 components in Earth, while *Lucy Liu* has a Taurus Moon. This makes these 3 stars the most grounded of the lot. *Miley Cyrus* has heavy Scorpio and Uranus aspects. Meanwhile, the Mutable Ascendants of *Stiller* (Gemini), *Elish* (Pisces) and *Jeff Bridges* (Virgo), greatly skew their facial lines. In contrast, *Bette Midler's* Cardinal Aries Ascendent straightens the lines of her Mutable Sun.

Achieve your highest goals, *with your CAPRICORN Friends!*

December 22 to January 19
(Dates vary slightly in some years)

Capricorn

Genesis: **Feminine Polarity, Cardinal Earth**

On the **Winter Solstice**, it is the shortest day of the year in the northern hemisphere.* Here, the Sun is starting its northward climb to the equator, to begin a new cycle of building light. *Everything is looking up*—when the Sun enters the Sign of **Capricorn**, and the chart's **4th Quadrant of integration.**

In this month, societies around the world are reviewing their actions in the previous 12 months, as they celebrate the New Year ahead! It is here where they make the resolutions and future actions—that *will bring everything together,* to create and support the new forms of life, that will come in the Spring!

*... and the longest day in the Southern Half.

More than other Signs, Capricorns are keenly aware of the importance of Time. That is why these tenacious goats think long range, and they rarely give up on any of their goals.

Fields of Likely Location:
The Goat climbs to the top of the mountain

When Capricorns make their climb to success, they calculate every step. With their perseverance and self-discipline, they often achieve their goals. For many of these goats, the work never ends—for their "mission of service" (inspired earlier by sister Earth Sign **Virgo**) drives them to build the efficient and long lasting institutions, that will hopefully solve the material needs for future generations.

Young Capricorns can be found in low-end cafes and at the local thrift store. At mid-life, they may serve in social organizations and on political councils—as they climb the social ladder! In later years, after they achieve a sense of success, they may dine at the finer establishments and wear expensive clothes. The wiser goats realize that these material accruements are not the true indicators of success—for they believe that *all things need to do well*—since *real* security comes from the conditions in places, far beyond our homes. They know that without functioning communities and nations—no individuals will be secure! Notably, this base of security begins in the home in the Sign of **Cancer**, Capricorn's opposing Sign.

With all of this, some goats become overwhelmed by our failed institutions and human foibles. They become bitter and cynical, as they lose their sense of direction and purpose. Others become incredibly cheap and obsessed with acquiring their own wealth and power. To affirm a higher hope in humanity, such individuals must focus on the altruistic beliefs of **Aquarius**—the next Sign in the Zodiac.

Associations: **Ruling Planet ~ Saturn** (Traditionally, also rules Aquarius)

Before the discovery of Uranus, Saturn ruled **Capricorn** and also **Aquarius**. Today, Saturn is still associated with limitation and restriction—a condition assigned, since it was enclosed by its rings and it was *the last* visible planet. Also, this planet's 29.5 year cycle represents **Father Time**, for its 7+ year transit over each of the chart's four Cardinal points marks "the four stages of aging" in a person's life.

Saturn represents the crystallization process, that turns water (and all other elements) into structured form. In Roman lore, Saturn was the god of agriculture and the founder of civilizations and social order. This planet is also associated with the teeth and bones (the solid structure that shapes our bodies). Saturn also rules aging and the long term planning that a person constructs in his or her life.

More than others, Capricorn careers are often defined by the components near the MC, or in the **10th House**. They make excellent managers, consultants and teachers. Any career receives 110% effort.

Physical Traits: Capricorn rules the knees

The force of **Cardinal Earth** is contained in the knees, the body part ruled by **Capricorn**. These bony joints enable us all—to physically move beyond our **Cancer** homes and explore distance outreaches on the Earth!

With the knees to the front, the feet are planted firmly on the ground. With each cautious step, the goat climbs steadily upward—to the mountain peaks above! With these mechanics, the protruding knees send the thighs and butt to the back. This tilts the upper torso and head forward. This angle points the head down to the ground. The eyes are aimed upward, so that the goat can see the craggy peaks, that lie above.

The size of this goat's body parts are often minimized by the consolidating force of Saturn. The goat's extremities, like those of the crab, are unusually thin. Unlike the crab's large shelled torso, Capricorn's upper chest is flat, and the shoulders are lean and bony.

The illustration on the previous page, shows how the goat's wide-set and beady eyes wrap to the sides, as they rest over the broad and high set cheek bones. This forms caverns below the eyes and it accounts for their serious appearance. Below, the goat's nostrils rest high above the extra large and tall upper lip plate.

These images of *Faye Dunaway* and *James Earl Jones* show how their thin upper lips (and tight drawn mouths) make their upper lip plates appear larger than normal. Both of them have Capricorn Suns and Moons. James' Capricorn Ascendant gives this triple Earth Sign his deep and resonant voice. These bony goat-like features can also be seen in the Capricorns below.

Eddy Vedder and *Greta Thunberg* display the serious demeanor, we often see in younger goats. *Betty White* reveals how they mellow and appear younger with age. *Judd Law, Michelle Obama* and *Christiane Amanpour* show how the high-set cheekbones and the cavern below the eyes, gives these goats their serious appearance.

This rigid face, the down-turned nose and the large pointed ears of the goat are seen in *Ben Kingsley, Ted Danson* and *John Legend*. Legend's Capricorn Ascendant accounts for his high and wide cheek bones. Danson's Virgo Ascendant makes his face longer than the others. In the sparkling crystal eyes of *Sissy Spacek,* we see the contentment of a soul, who has reached the top of her mountain.

Intuitively, *AQUARIUS* knows what needs to be known.

Aquarius
January 20 to February 18
Genesis: Masculine Polarity, Fixed Air

On the dates above, the Sun is midway on its northbound journey to the equator. In the northern hemisphere, it's **Mid-Winter** and all around the world the **Fixed Air** Sign of **Aquarius** is behind the morning Sun. This rising light confirms to all: *The skies are getting brighter every day!*

With these brightening rays of hope, individuals are inspired to invent an array of new ideas—to complete last month's New Year's resolutions—and make the future even brighter!

Unlike the opposing Sign of **Leo**, Aquariuses are oriented to the future, rather than in the present moment. This "focus on the future" may be why they are always late for their appointments.

This "orientation to the future" drives Aquariuses to correct the outdated thinking of others. With this "fixing", they believe that their ideas will inspire the revolution that will take down **Capricorn**'s failed institutions—and raise the hopes of humanity!

Fields of Likely Location:
With mental concentration, revolutionary ideals manifest

The Fixed Air minds of Aquarius make them incredibly intuitive—and very capable of tuning into the *Akashi Records*—the place where all past, present and future thoughts are stored. Recent theories also contend that the *Element of Water* can conduct and store the vibrational information in its surroundings. Perhaps the ancients knew that years ago, and that's why Aquariuses are called *"The Water Bearers"*.

Individuals with an Aquarius Sun, Moon or Rising Sign (or a strongly aspected Uranus) often express the qualities of Fixed Air, and an array of outrageous ideas. That's why you may find your Aquarius friends at UFO and New Age gatherings, pitching radical concepts, or gathering funds for humanitarian projects.

Many of these cosmic cowboys (and cowgirls) are rarely connected to earthy things, since their minds are fixed onto the intuitive messages, that are constantly popping into their heads. The downside is that this mental focus makes it difficult for these Water Bearers to express their emotions and feelings.

To complete the *4th Quadrant's Process of Integration*, all of the previous efforts must be merged together—to form the seeds for a new beginning. This final step is the task for the last Sign in the Zodiac: **Pisces**.

Associations: Ruling Planet~Uranus (Traditionally also ruled by Saturn)

Originally, **Saturn** was the co-ruler of Aquarius and Capricorn. After this planet's discovery in 1781, astrologers made **Uranus** the ruler of Aquarius. Since the circulatory system delivers *"sustaining waters"* to the body, it was also assigned to be ruled by Uranus. This planet is also associated with space travel, aeronautics, mass communication and works of science fiction.

Aquarius is ruled by the planet Uranus. These Uranian energies suggest the function of a capacitor—a device that stores electricity. When its capacity is filled, the switch is triggered and its power is abruptly released in a concentrated outburst of electrons. Likewise, Uranus' position in the sky can bring unexpected electrical and neurological changes. Uranus also gives us the eccentric and independent thinkers, who often excel as scientists, social workers, writers and reporters in the field of mass communication.

Physical Traits: Aquarius rules the Calves, Lower Leg & Circulatory System

When the force of Fixed Air is concentrated in the calves and lower legs, the lower quadrant of the body is pulled to the front, as the torso and arms lag to the back. Watch how the calves flap in the breeze and how the feet rarely touch the ground, when Aquarius skips above the ground like a hovercraft!

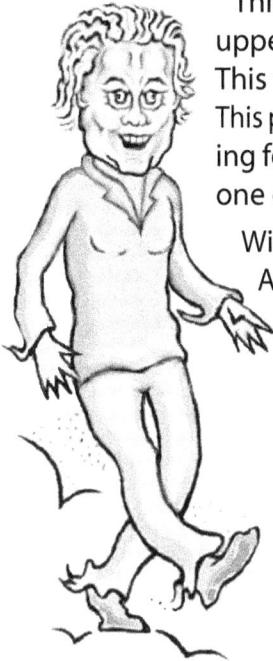

This body rulership also defines Aquarius' body physique. Save for the large head, the upper half appears to be normal in its width, but rather flat in its front-to-back dimensions. This flattening starts at the hips and it becomes more obvious, as it progresses upward. This phenomenon of Fixed Air is like a sail—it tightens and widens, as it captures the incoming forces of wind! All the while, the calves are longer than normal. This makes Aquarius one of the "top four" tallest Signs in the Zodiac.

With his Aquarius Sun and Ascendant, *Michael C. Hall* shows how the facial elements of Aquarius are compacted into a small area on the face. This compaction draws the cheek bones inward, as it pulls the jaw upward. This creates the square face, that appears flat in depth. It also creates the tight-lipped smiles we see in the images below.

This centering of facial components draws the eyelids inward, to create the highly recognizable hooded eyes of Aquarius.

With her Aquarius Sun and Rising Sign, *Charlotte Rampling* was given her unique billowing eyelids. With them, and her sparkling eyes, she stood out from the crowd—and it made her a star!

Carol Channing, *Farrah Fawcett* and *Geena Davis* do not have the "flat square face" of Aquarius. Instead, their eyes are slightly skewed and their rectangular jaws project out from the upper half of the face. Their Suns are all in the Gemini decant. [The effects of decants are illustrated in the next section].

Alicia Keys and *Justin Timberlake,* with their Mutable Sagittarius Risings, display the long protruding jaw of a horse. *Ted Koppel, Neil Diamond* and *Ellen DeGeneres* show how Aquarius' facial components occupy a relatively small area of the face. Justin joins Ellen, to demonstrate how Aquarius' distantly focused eyes seem to look right through you—as if you weren't even there. Lastly, we have *Alan Alda* and *Tom Selleck*, who show the solid personas of their Capricorn Ascendants and Fixed Moons.

Dreams come true, with the help of *your PISCES Friends!*

Pisces
February 19 to March 20
(Dates vary slightly in some years)

Genesis: Feminine Polarity, Mutable Water

When the Sun enters **Pisces**, it is the last month of Winter in the northern hemisphere. Everyday, the morning light of the purple-hued Pisces Sun rises in the East—to melt the snows and wet the world with the universal solvent.

To wrap up the chart's **4th Quadrant of Integration**, the directives of **Capricorn** and the insightful resolutions of **Aquarius** are submerged in the swirling waters of **Pisces**. In these Mutable Waters, all of the lessons of the previous year are blended in Nature's magical brew. This forms the seeds for the new birth of life, that will appear in the Spring—when the Sun enters the Sign of **Aries**.

Fields of Likely Location:
In pools of reflecting lights, the fish gratefully swims

When these fish swim in their sea of swirling currents, the sparkle of reflecting lights quickly attracts their attentions. Is that flashing light a lure to entice them to take a bite? If it feels right, will they take the leap? Or—if it feels wrong—will they avoid it at all costs? Such feelings are complicated, perhaps that is why some of our Pisces friends appear so indecisive. Why not? *They are feeling everything!*

In all of the pools of humanity, you will find these timid souls. They may be the nurses who care for injured patients, or the "soft-spoken" and often unrecognized committee members—who stir the feelings of others, with their compassionate observations. With their quiet strength, Pisceans have a gift for transforming the collective desires, sensations, thoughts and feelings of others—as they inspire them to join all of the others in their "school of fish"—so that we can swim together as One, in perfect synchronicity!

With their joyful feelings, Pisceans counter the worrisome and critical thinking of **Virgo**—the opposite Sign in the Zodiac. Still, Virgo is there to remind us: *Things are never perfect* and dreaming does not complete the work that is needed, to be of service to others. Miraculously, when both of these Signs operate in unity, there is a "melding of feelings with the mind". **This sparks the imagination!** All of us can now believe that anything is possible!

Since we are a product of the cycles in Nature, it is clear that bits of each of the 12 Signs are in all of us—guiding our spirits, bodies, minds and feelings. Their placement can tell us of the talents that each of us were given, as they give us hints of the course of events in our lives. This knowing helps all of us to find our connection with the divine creative force that runs throughout the Universe. It will likely be a Pisces friend, who will help you to make this magical connection.

Associations: Ruling Planet ~ Neptune (Traditionally, also Jupiter)

When the long-range waves of Neptune interweave with the shortwave patterns of one's mental and emotional frequencies—imaginative images appear! Anything that enhances or distorts one's feelings and perceptions is under the control of Neptune. Hospitals (healing), poetry, dancing and religious inspiration are positive Neptune creations. Insanity, poisons and prisons lurk on the darker side. Here, the services offered in **Virgo** are now completed. Our actions bring their karmic consequences. What we have given is what we will receive in return.

Careers for Pisces Suns include dancers, actors, poets, artists, fishermen and priests. Their vivid imaginations have given us the scientific discoveries of *Albert Einstein* and *Linus Pauling*, the delightful fantasies of *Dr. Suess* and the spiritual insights of *Edgar Cayce*. They show us that every dream is possible!

Physical Traits ~ Pisces rules the Feet

When body rulership drops into the feet, the *nerve meridians* in each foot connect to all parts of the body. These circuits cycle Pisces' healing forces on the left and right side of the body—upward, back to the **Aries**-ruled head. With each step, a certain desire, sensation, thought and/or feeling is stimulated, as Pisces meanders down their path of destiny.

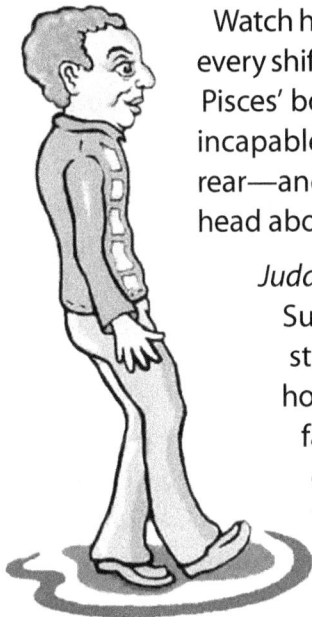

Watch how their bodies bob up and down, like flotsam on the ocean's surface—and how every shift in the ocean currents alters their course of direction. This body rulership defines Pisces' body language and physique. With their feet paddling to the front, the Fish seems incapable of pursuing a forward assault. Note how the upper body is weighted to the rear—and how it bulges at the upper back. This is the life preserver, that keeps Pisces' head above the waterline.

Judd Hirsch and *Lynn Redgrave* (with their Pisces Suns and Ascendants) show the skewed bone structure and facial lines of mutability. Note how the bubbly flesh swells on one side of the face, as it deflates on the other. This division often matches the tilted angle between the two eyes—and It gives these fish the portal view, that enables them to see both sides of everything, in their dreamy world.

The currents of **Mutable Water** vary in these Pisces Sun Signs. The large dreamy eyes of *Albert Einstein* and *Ruth Banner Ginzberg* allowed them to see the universal truths in physics and in the laws of the land.

Joanne Woodword, Steve Irwin and *George Harrison* reflect the look of wonder, that comes when one is connected to the spirits of all things big and small. *Drew Barrymore* and *Jennifer Love Hewitt* demonstrate the "waveform in the eyes", that is formed when one eyelid rises upward on the outer side, and the other lid drops downward on the outer edge. *Queen Latifa, Dr. Suess* and *Michael Caine* show how their fish-like eyes peer off in two portal directions. This phenomenon appears in the faces of many Pisces.

59

☾ Celebrities with Common Moon Signs

With the Moon's monthly orbit around the Earth, a new Sign appears every 2 1/2 days behind the Moon. The Sign in which the Moon is placed (at our birth) dictates our "reactive nature"—or how we emotionally interact to the events, conditions and people we encounter. This lunar interaction often attempts to support our personal sense of comfort, as it defines the space that we call "home".

Here, using groups of different Sun Signs, we will show the reactions of celebrities who share a common Moon. As noted in our discussion on the Moon (page 23), this reaction changes one's facial expression, as it renders the Mode and Element of one's Moon Sign. The images in this section should help you to identify the reactions of each of the Moon Signs.

Aries Moon Signs

Whatever one's Sun Sign, the Cardinal Fire of an **Aries Moon** often brings strongly-driven emotional reactions. These fiery Moons are quick to temper, but fortunately, their tantrums also quickly subside.

When **AQUARIUS** *Ellen DeGeneres* becomes emotional, her lunar reactions are forceful and highly directed. Without hesitation, every idea in her head is instantly cast out, often without considering the feelings of others.

TAURUS *Cate Blanchett* is very practical in her career choices, but with her Moon and Venus in Aries, she is emotionally comfortable playing warrior queen and action roles. It's what we saw in "*Elizabeth*" and "*Indiana Jones*".

GEMINI *Anderson Cooper*'s Aries Moon keeps his thoughts on track, as he plows through the verbal clutter on his CNN cable show. His questions are often well aimed—and to the point!

SAGITTARIUS *Kiefer Sutherland*'s Aries Moon opposes his Mars. This gives him the short-fused temper, that in his younger days led to his multiple arrests for brawling and accosting others.

With this Libra Rising and a Moon-ruled Sun, **CANCER** *Benedict Cumberbatch* rarely shows any outward aggression—until someone questions this thoughts and feelings—then look out!

Pink (Aleica Beth Moore) is not a worrywart **VIRGO**. She's a lady of action, who aggressively pursued her recording career. She even proposed to her future husband.

Taurus Moon Signs

Taurus Moons are the opposite of Aries, since their reactions mock the nature of Fixed Earth. In their emotional moments, all things goes on hold!

In their fiery expressions, **LEO** *Delta Burke* and **SAGITTARIUS** *Bill Nye* often become surprisingly silent—and momentarily lost for words, when their Fixed Earth emotions take control. Well, at least for a second or two.

ARIES *William Shatner* and **GEMINI** *Bob Dylan* lose all traces of their Cardinal and Mutable natures, when their emotions are aroused. With four components in Taurus, Dylan's actions are incredibly grounded, even with his Mutable Sun and Sagittarius Ascendant.

With her Venus-ruled Libra Sun, Taurus Ascendant and Moon—few would guess *Sigourney Weaver* to be a easy going LIBRA. With Pluto on her Leo Mars (as we saw in "*Alien*"), his tough lady keeps everything in control.

CANCER *Meryl Streep*'s lunar reactions show little of the fixity we see in the others. That is because her Sun Sign is ruled by the Moon. The Cardinal tides of her Sun liquefy and round her earthy lunar reactions.

Gemini Moon Signs

Gemini Moons rarely appear emotional or sentimental. They usually release their emotions by talking and verbally interacting with others. Their mercuric chatter often increases when others react to their comments. **ARIES** *Jackie Chan* may be a master of martial arts, but look at what happens, when he gets cornered: He starts to chatter!

This same phenomenon happens with TV host **TAURUS** *Stephen Colbert*. When he appears to lose control of any situation, he quickly reacts by interrupting others, with his cheeky, verbal counter reactions.

In her TV show, we saw how the normally unflappable personality of SCORPIO *Roseanne Barr* would unravel, when her Gemini emotions took control. There, her voice would take on an irritatingly high pitch—and her hands would fly about, to animate her martial Scorpio feelings. Others appear to have more restrained lunar reactions: President *Barrack Obama*, with his fixed **LEO** Sun and **Aquarius** Rising, kept his mutable emotions under control. In emotional moments, he became extra "wordy".

LIBRA *Barbara Walters,* the former newswoman and host of *"The View",* was known for her calmness and friendly batter. However, unlike Obama, she did not become more wordy, her speed of speech would just increase.

This reflection of mental "air forces" was also seen in **AQUARIUS** *Jane Seymour*'s TV show *"Dr. Quinn, Medicine Woman"*. There, Jane's simple conversations would quickly become lengthy and complex dialogues on various subjects, ranging from health to social issues.

Cancer Moon Signs

Since Cancer is ruled by the Moon, you are likely to see a tidal surge of emotions, when one of these "Children of the Moon" reacts to another.

ARIES *Emma Thompson* and **LEO** *Halle Berry* can be fiery in their cinematic performances, but they're also known for their skills at expressing powerful inner emotions. In such moments, their expansive Aries fires turn inward to create the internal pressure, that inflates their facial flesh. Externally, their emotions often erupt in a tide of emotions, or in a flood of tears.

With a mercuric **VIRGO** Sun and Ascendant, *Keanu Reeves*' emotions rarely rise to the surface. However, when his tidal waters are activated, watch how his face swells—to create his round "Full Moon" temples. He shows how the Moon's rulership of Cancer strongly alters the features of one's Sun Sign.

GEMINI *Mike Myers* uses his crabby lunar emotions (and the contrasting qualities to his expansive, analytical Sun) to create his outrageous comedy. Watch him in his moments of emotional insecurity, and how his mercuric chatter abruptly ceases, as his flying hands clutch tightly to his chest.

With **TAURUS** *Willy Nelson*, this lunar placement gives us a person with an earthy, soothing voice—and an ingrained sense of rhythm. His water Moon keeps the music flowing, at a steady, orchestrated cadence.

Liza Minnelli shows us how the emotions of a wavering **PISCES** Sun are pushed and pulled by the tides of a surging Cardinal Water Moon. This combination of watery expressions gave her a liquid and emotional voice, and a highly driven imagination.

Leo Moon Signs

Most people (with prominent Leo components) shine brightly in any role. This theatrical flair is enhanced in the emotional reactions of those who have a Leo Moon. These lunar feelings often bring boastful reactions and a wonderful sense of playfulness and self-confidence.

LIBRA *Bruno Mars* and VIRGO *Amy Poehler* show us what happens, when their lion emotions take control. In those moments, the patterns of their Cardinal and Mutable Suns become fixed. This gives them the confidence to place themselves on center stage !

In her showy performance in *"Chicago"*, *Queen Latifa* showed little of the timid qualities of her PISCES Sun. It was the Fixed Fire of her Leo Moon that gave her gave her the feeling that "she was royalty". [See Snapshot, pg. 94]

AQUARIUS *Tom Selleck* was the free-spirited detective in TV's original *"Magnum, P.I."* and the head of Police in his role in *"Blue Bloods"*. In both roles, his eyebrows would rise and his chest would swell, when he received compliments from others. When you praise anyone with a Leo Moon, you'll see the same reaction.

When CANCER *Tom Hanks* interacts with others, he holds his head high and anchors himself in place, as he shows his Sun's concern for others. In his responses, he shows how Leo Moons can be incredibly generous.

The self-confidence of Fixed Fire is seen in the *solar projections* of LEO *Charlize Theron*—and also in her *Lunar reactions*. This accounts for the theatrical intensity that we saw in her role as the serial murderer in *Monster*, and her action roles in *Atomic Blonde* and the two *Mad Max* films.

Virgo Moon Signs

Virgo Moons usually show little emotion. They remain cool, as they try to calculate a practical solution to any emotional situation. When they sense that things are out of order, they become noticeably nervous.

Natalie Portman has a GEMINI Sun and Virgo Moon. That explains why (early in her career), she once said: "I don't care if college ruins my career. I'd rather be smart than a movie star." That resoluteness comes from her Virgo Moon. The urge to study was driven by her Mars and Sun in Gemini.

LEO *J.K. Rowling* has three components and her Virgo Moon in Mutable Earth. With this giant mercuric input, Rowling found words to help youngsters discover their personal creative and expressive powers.

TAURUS *Jack Nicholson* and SCORPIO *Jodi Foster* also have fixed Suns, and like Rowling, their cubical and fixed solar features are skewed by the mercuric force of their Virgo Moons. In his interactions, Jack proceeds to criticize the imperfections in his physical surroundings. Jodi's Virgo emotions appear to shield her in a protective shield of purity, that often appears to distance her from any close emotional involvements.

With a grand water trine between his CANCER Sun and Ascendant and his Saturn and Jupiter, the *Dali Lama* has an amazing ability to connect with the feelings of others. With his Virgo Moon conjoined Neptune, he easily finds the right words, to help others pursue their spiritual paths.

With his mercuric Moon, actor ARIES *James Franco* is also fascinated with acquiring "knowledge and data". He once took 62 course credits at UCLA in one quarter. The normal course load is around 19. He still got a 4.00 GPA.

Libra Moon Signs

In the world of entertainment, celebrities usually attempt to present a pleasant and non-offensive image to their public. It is easy, when they react with the cherub-like smiles of their **Libra Moons**.

ARIES *Alex Baldwin* shows us how the long face of the Ram is stretched horizontally by the **Cardinal Force** of Libra. With this Moon, the martial force of Aries disappears as it is replaced by Alex's wide-spread smile.

With **CAPRICORN** *Bradley Cooper*, the emotional input of his Venus-ruled Cardinal Moon gives him the esthetic insights, to pursue his work as an actor, writer, director and motion picture producer.

When the lunar forces of Libra are activated in the **Fixed Sun Signs**, the physical changes are more obvious. *Anne Hatcher* shows how her tight, fixed smile and the intense eyes of her **SCORPIO** Sun spread to the sides—when she reacts with her Libra Moon.

In **AQUARIUS** *Alicia Keys*' emotional moments, the focused features of her airy Sun dissipate, to reform into Libra's pleasant smile. In the process, her cool and high-pitched voice becomes soft and melodic.

The effects of a Libra Moon are also clear in the **Mutable Signs**. GEMINI *Annette Bening* shows us how the skewed facial lines rearrange, to reveal the perfectly balanced reactions of her Moon.

Not so, with **VIRGO** *Bob Newhart*, for it was the indecisiveness of his Libra Moon—and the fussiness of his overly-critical Sun—that enabled him to perfect his highly successful, four decade long comedy routine.

Scorpio Moon Signs

The Fixed Water of a Scorpio Moon often adds a moody intensity and a powerful aura of mystery to one's emotional reactions. This change in mode is easily seen in Mutable Sun Signs.

VIRGO *Beyonce Knowles*' Scorpio emotions warm up the mercuric and earthy nature of her Sun. This Moon also adds depth, richness and a steamy quality to her voice.

When *Alan Rickman's fixed emotions rise to the surface,* his eyes take on a laser-like intensity. However, with the shifting waters of his PISCES Sun, the hold is quickly broken—and the secrets are revealed for all to see!

This change in mode is also seen in the Cardinality of **Lady GaGa**'s Mars-ruled ARIES Sun. Notably, since Mars rules her Sun and traditionally also her Moon, she has a gift for manifesting an array of macabre and dark creative works. [See her Snapshot on page 86].

This hold on the Cardinal drive is also seen in Libra *Snoop Dog*. Watch how his charming smile dissapears, when his emotions are activated.

In most folks with Fixed Sun Signs and Moons, there is no modal change, when they are expressing themselves or reactioning to others. This is seen in *Mila Kunis*, an actress who has a fixed Leo Sun and Mars.

Sagittarius Moon Signs

Individuals with Sagittarius Moons have few emotional attachments. Many feel they are free to pursue any impulse that they desire.

The emotional responses of the Fire and Air Signs are instant. As we see in the double fire of **LEO** *Hilary Swank*, her fiery lunar reactions instantly skew and exaggerates her facial expressions.

With **AQUARIUS** *Oprah Winsfrey*, the force of her Mutable Moon also skews her facial expressions, but the twists are less exaggerated. This may be due to the five Fixed components in her chart.

Gemini *Nicole Kidman*'s solar and lunar lights are both driven by the force of Mutability. With her Moon being the most aspected component in her chart, her moods instantly change and often appear erratic.

In the passive Earth and Water Sun Signs, the lunar fires of a Centaur Moon are rarely contained, even in the Fixed Earth of **TAURUS** *Al Pacino*. Though his Sun is the "most grounded Sign", when he becomes emotional, the fires of his Sagittarius Moon quickly flare to the surface.

With **CAPRICORN** *John Legend*, such exuberance is rarely seen. This is due to his Mars and Sun's conjunction on his Capricorn Ascendent. He appears to keep his emotions under control, most of the time.

With his Mutable Water Sun (and expansive lunar reactions), **PISCES** *Albert Einstein* was given the gift to *see and feel* the universal creative process, that operated in sub-atomic particles and also in the galaxies above.

Capricorn Moon Signs

Let's get serious folks—the Moon has moved into Capricorn!

PISCES *Ron Howard*'s Capricorn Moon's makes him task-oriented and determined to "get things done". The meandering emotions of his Pisces Sun were kept on track by his Cardinal Moon. This made him one of Hollywood's most successful film directors and producers.

CANCER *Anthony Bourdain* showed his fascination with cooking in this TV show "*Unknown Parts*". With his two Cardinal luminaries, he was driven to travel around the world, to explore the cuisines of different cultures.

The emotions of the **Earth Sun Signs** are more contained. *George Cloony* often projects the relaxed image of his contented **TAURUS Sun**. However, when he is placed in a dire situation—as we saw in his role in *The Perfect Storm*—his emotions hardened, when he needed to regain control.

VIRGO *Taraji P. Henson* shows few of the Mutable traits of her Sun. With her Moon's grand trine to her Sun and Capricorn's ruler Saturn, she was given the emotional toughness to play the lead role in TV's "*Empire*".

With her two Cardinal luminaries (and her Moon's trine to her Mars), **ARIES** *Sarah Jessica Parker* made her climb to the top, finding success in her TV show "*Sex in the City*" and on Broadway. It was her Aries Sun that drove her to run full speed ahead—and it was her Capricorn Moon that gave her the tenacity to persist and succeed.

Aquarius *Mia Farrow*'s Moon and Mars are in Capricorn. In most of her interactions with others, the stern force of Cardinal Earth often appears, when it needs to support her frequent disagreements with others.

Aquarius Moon Signs

When the Moon skips into Aquarius, many people feel a sense of hope and optimism. Others feel that it's time to instill a little chaos.

GEMINI *Marilyn Monroe*'s **Leo Ascendant** made her incredibly attractive to everyone. Consequently, few recognized the intelligence that she was given by her airy Sun and Moon. Sadly, her emotionally distancing Moon also made her incapable of finding any meaningful emotional connections.

The fires of *Conan O'Brien's ARIES SUN* rarely subside, since they are constantly feed oxygen by his Aquarius Moon. Watch how his facial elements are pulled into the center, when he pulls a "punch line" from out of the blue.

With the **Water Sun Signs**, Aquarius Moons often brings unexpected emotional reactions. **CANCER** *Willem Defoe* is known for his many eccentric and villainous roles. This extraordinary talent is likely due to the fact that Mars, Jupiter and Uranus conjoin his Sun.

In her tour de force performance in "*Fatal Attraction*", *PISCES Glenn Close's* emotions shifted from compassionate to freakish frightening. She showed how one's mind could become consumed by its own mental fixations.

Aquarius Moons make **Earth Sun Signs** *delightfully eccentric.*

VIRGO Bill Murray is determined to be helpful to everyone he encounters. If there is any resistance, he quickly become fixated on "correcting the problem". His erratic emotional reactions often make the problem worse.

TAURUS Uma Thurman often shows the contented qualities of her earthy Sun, but her Virgo Ascendant T-squares Mars and Neptune. She can appear as a warrior foe or a supporting friend. It will be her quixotic emotional beliefs, that will decide which side she's on.

Pisces Moon Signs

Imagine emotions that are all-inclusive and all encompassing. Everything goes into the wash, when the Moon slips into the sloshing waters of Pisces.

TAURUS *Jerry Seinfeld* bragged his show was about "nothing", which means it could also be about "everything". Nothing becomes everything, when a compassionate Pisces Moon reacts to its surroundings.

When **SCORPIO** *Hillary Clinton* told us "It takes a Village", she meant it— for under the surface, she has a compassionate Pisces Moon. This Moon served her well in her diplomatic role as Secretary of State. The public could not see this compassion, all they saw was her secretive and controlling Sun.

With **LIBRA** *Joan Cusack* and **ARIES** *Rachel Maddow*, the Cardinal drive of their solar natures subside, when they are inundated by the emotions of their Water Moons. This inflow of water inflates their bubbly flesh, as it transforms the expressions in their faces. When Rachel's Pisces Moon glows behind her anchor's chair, her stories often become touching and filled with feeling.

When **LEO** *Steve Carel* and **SAGITTARIUS** *Ben Stiller* interact with others, their feelings bubble to the surface. This douses the fires of their Suns as it quiet the voices of their normally loud and boisterous personalities.

Carel's Moon has 7 major aspects including a conjunction to Jupiter. This gives him his excitable personality, and his gift for creating his comic fantasies. In contrast, Stiller's Moon is conjoined by Saturn. Unlike Carel, his emotions are cool, controlled and often far more serious.

Celebrities with Common Ascendants

On page 26, this book discussed how the Earth's daily rotation places another one of the planet's 360 vertical longitudinal lines on the eastern horizon. The Sun does not change its position, but the Sign on the eastern horizon changes around every 2.5 hours. If you calculate the hourly differences between your time-of-birth and sunrise, it is easy to approximate the Sign that is was "rising" in your chart.

This Ascendant defines our expectations for the day, as it colors how we see the world, every day in our lives. This Rising Sign greatly influences the skeletal structure, as it shapes the image that is initially seen by others. It stands out front, when a person is not projecting the light of his/her Sun.

Aries Ascendants

When **Aries** rises in the morning light, the Cardinal Fires light the path for the day ahead. Aries Ascendants charge down this path at *full speed ahead*.

Libra *John Lennon*'s was the most aggressive member of *The Beatles*. It was the solar urges of his Libra Sun, that inspired him to "give peace a chance", but this message was forcefully directed out through his Ascendant. He became the leader of the band—that gave direction to a generation!

TAURUS *Barbara Streisand* is known for her insistence on controlling every level of her creative work. This controlling urge comes from her Sun. The path for her creative endeavors was driven by her fiery Ascendant.

SCORPIO *Helen Reddy*, like Streisand, combines Fixity and Cardinality. Both ladies show little of the cubical shaping of a Fixed Sun. Instead, we see the arched eyebrows, the prominent snout and the convex bone structure on the front of the vertically stretched "ram face".

In the Mutable Suns of **GEMINI** *Morgan Freeman*, **VIRGO** *James Coburn* and **SAGITTARIUS** *Bette Midler*, the convex facial structure of the Ram is strong, but the facial elements appear skewed. For Morgan and James, their personalities are less mercuric than what we'd expect from their Mercury-ruled Suns. With her double fire, Midler is the most rambunctious of this group.

Taurus Ascendants

When Taurus rises in the east, Fixed Earth forces reign. Here, the Earth of *Halle Berry's* **Taurus Ascendant** grounds the fires of her **LEO Sun** and **Moon**. Being a triple Fixed Sign, Halle shows the cubical features of fixity—and the mixed features of a Lion and a Bull!

ARIES *Wiliam Shatner* also has a stocky build, but his Sun makes his eyes sheepish, rather than bovine in nature. This Cardinal Fire of his Sun was more obvious, when he took command of the *Starship Enterprise*.

The rest of our subjects are Mutable Sun Signs. These images, likely taken in their moments of "repose", show little of the skewed features of Mutability.

PISCES *Queen Latifa's* overpowering presence in the movie "**Chicago**" was likely fired up by her Leo Moon. Her massive physical appearance, broad shoulders and stocky body structure are a product of her Ascendant

Physically, **GEMINI** *Salman Rushdie* shows few of the lean and lanky qualities of Mutable Air. However, his Gemini is seen in his mastery of words, and in his animated hands, when he "details" the thoughts in his mind.

SAGITTARIUSES *Brendan Fraser* and *Myley Cyrus* both lack the long jaw and high forehead of the Centaur. Brendan's Venus-ruled Ascendant is enhanced by his Taurus Moon and four Venus aspects. (This accounts for his relaxed and "sleepy" appearance). Myley's Scorpio Moon adds intensity to her eyes. Her Venus' conjunction to Uranus explains her quirky antics.

Gemini Ascendants

At some point in every day, the Earth will have the Sun rising in the Sign of Gemini. In that moment of time, great ideas are stirring!

When *Matthew McConaughey's* SCORPIO Sun is inactive, his skewed and twisted bone structure is revealed. In these moments, the mercuric forces of Gemini rise to the surface. This gives him a gift of gab.

With CAPRICORN *John Denver*, the Gemini winds loosened the granite qualities of his Sun. With his Ascendant's trine to Neptune, he found the words and the music, that took him to the top of the mountain.

With her GEMINI mask and VIRGO Moon, TAURUS *Michelle Pfieffer* has a light, sparkling and mercuric personae. These two mercuric components give her qualities that hint more of Virgo, than those of Fixed Earth.

LEOS *Sandra Bullock* and *Mick Jagger* show how the bone structure of Gemini shifts the lower half of the face forward, while it also twists and angles the cubical features, that are common in most Lions.

Notably, Jagger's Sun, Jupiter and Uranus conjoin his Ascendant. Jagger puts on a dazzlingly show. With Mars and Venus on her mercuric Ascendant, Sandra finds strength articulating her ideas, thru her use of language.

Another Fire Sign is ARIES *Lady GaGa*. Her large Ram snout and uplifted eyebrows remain, but her slewed eyes and jaw reveal the mutability of her Gemini Ascendant. She also shows Gemini's large, front "rabbit teeth" —and how they angle off from a normal vertical alignment.

Cancer Ascendants

When Cancer rises in the morning light, the Summer Solstice's shift into waning light is felt everywhere, at the break of dawn.

With their Cancer Ascendants, VIRGO *Stephen King* and SCORPIO *Joni Mitchell* display the round temples of the crab. King shows few of the lines of mutability, while Joni's round bone structure masks the intense qualities of her Sun.

LEO *Robert DeNiro*'s Cancer mask is dramatized by his Sun, and it's all exaggerated by his Pisces Moon. This combination of components gave him an ability to project toughness, as well as emotional vulnerability.

TAURUS *Adele* shows the large bovine eyes of her Sun, but the underlying bone structure of Cancer is rounding the earthy edges and inflating her flesh. The cubical features of Fixed Earth are hard to detect.

GEMINI *Angelina Jolie* shows us how the angles of a Mutable Sun are straightened by the force of a Cardinal Ascendant. Her eyes and jaw are still tilted and slightly out of kilter, but in the center, her bone structure reveals the round lunar temples of the crab.

SAGITTARIUS *Steven Spielberg* rarely shows the excited personality for a Centaur. Note how his high domed forehead and bulbous nose provides hints of his Sun, while the bubbly flesh and inflated features present the timid presence of a Cancer Crab.

67

It was the positioning of this watery Rising Sun, that enabled Steven to arouse the emotions of others in his amazingly films. In *Jaws*, he stroked our fears for being in the water. *Indiana Jones* captured the adventure of his Centaur Sun, while *ET* touched our families with it wonder and fantasy.

Leo Ascendants

When morning's light is in Leo, the expectations for the day are glorious and magnificent! For Leo Ascendants, this vision prevails throughout the year.

In the passive Earth and Water Signs, the fires of the Lion usually do not roar as loud, but they still attract a lot of attention:

With **TAURUS** *Jessica Lange*, the sensual qualities of her Sun are magnified by the rising presence of Leo. This also makes her fixed traits obvious.

With his theatrical personae, **CAPRICORN** *Muhammad ALI* shouted "I am the greatest"—when he became the champion of the world!

CANCER *Meryl Streep*'s waters are well contained and lit within, by the inner embers in her crustacean shell. With this lion mask, Meryl's showy theatrics flow in perfect cadence, as their driven by her Cardinal Sun.

When Leo is out front, individuals with their Suns in the expansive Fire and Air Elements find that it is easier, to project their solar desires out to others!

When **GEMINI** *Johnny Depp* holds up his Fixed Leo mask, it contains his scattered solar forces, and it also removes the skewed features of his Mutable Sun. It also tells us why his chatty Sun has an incredible aura of confidence.

When **SAGITTARIUS** *Tina Turner* struts onto the stage, the stirring fires of her Sun are fed by the Air of her Gemini Moon. These two Mutable Forces are proudly presented through the portal of her Lion Ascendant.

AQUARIUS *Justin Timberlake*'s wintery Sun is awakened every day with the summery spotlight of Leo in his heart. As a youngster, his Sun *believed* he could sang, dance and fulfill this calling. With this, his Aquarius beliefs became a reality.

Virgo Ascendants

In Virgo's morning light, and in the passage of every day, there is an acute awareness that the glow of Leo is dimming. With this, many people recognize that a lot of work needs to be done—to prepare the Earth for the many changes that will come in the new season ahead. For some, this instills a sense of worry.

*These tasks are analytically pursued by these thought-driven **Air Signs**:*

GEMINI *Dana Carvey*'s comedic characterization of "The Church Lady" captured how Mercury's obsession with details could be so irritating.

On the other hand, *Julie Andrews* presents the cheery charm of her **LIBRA** Sun. In her film *"Mary Poppins"*, we saw her singing in the kitchen, as she instructed others on how to get the work done!

*The need for perfection is less obvious in these **Fire Signs**:*

LEO *Madonna* shows the proud stance of a lion, but her Ascendant's underlying skeletal structure gives her the small chest, lanky body and long arms of Virgo. Like most Virgo risings, she have a noticeable gap between her two front teeth—a gap that was later corrected by modern dentistry.

ARIES *Conan O'Brien* is also self-confident, but he often appears uncomfortable in "his space". Watch how his Moon impels him to twitch and nervously pull at his tie, when others question his opinions.

Water and *Earth Suns* are noticeably altered by their Virgo Ascendants:

CANCER *Tom Hanks* has the round features of the crab, but when Virgo rises to the surface, his features become vertically stretched and skewed.

SCORPIO *K.D. Lang*'s Ascendant presents the "initial image" when she walks on stage, but what her fans really want to experience is her soul-wrenching voice, the one that is empowered by Pluto on her Ascendant!

Libra Ascendants

Everyday, **Libra** rises in the morning light, on some point on Earth—to bring a momentary balance between day and night. All those born in this moment, perceive that this balance needs to be maintained everyday, thru out the year!

The morning light of Libra gave a youthful *Britney Spears* the direction, to conquer the creative desires of her **SAGITTARIUS** Sun. Later, when this balance was lost, she became a wild horse, out of control. A few years later, the balance returned—to send this Centaur galloping in a new creative direction.

In the Air Signs, there is a desire to keep all of their thoughts in balance:

GEMINI Paula Abdul was a judge on "American Idol". With her Mutable Air Sun, she would rattle out a scattering of words—to describe the failures of many of the contestants. Shortly after, her thoughtful and pleasant Libra mask would rise to describe and compliment the contestant's successes.

With her Fixed **AQUARIUS** Sun, *Jennifer Annison* often appears to be aloof and distant. However, in her interaction with others, her charming Libra smile always rose to the surface—to make the conversation more friendly.

Earth and Water Sun Signs present calm and pleasant masks to others.

The emotions of the Water Signs *PISCES Jon Bon Jovi* and **CANCER** *Benedict Cumberbatch* are often covered by their wide-spread smiles.

Jovi shows the skewed lines of his Mutable Sun, but Cumberbatch's Cardinal Sun and Ascendant clearly spreads this features in a horizontal direction.

These horizontal lines also appear in **CAPRICORN** *Denzel Washington*'s face. His wide sunken "goat" cheekbones are uplifted by his V-shaped smile. With his earthy Sun, he appears to be the most grounded of the group.

Scorpio Ascendants

In the dark skies of Scorpio, things often do not appear so nice.

For many, it is difficult to believe that *Clint Eastwood* is a **GEMINI**. What we saw in his "*Spaghetti Western* and *Dirty Harry* films" was the intense persona of his **Scorpio Ascendant**, rather than the light and mercuric energies of his Sun.

With the galloping filly **SAGITTARIUS** *Nicole Kidman*, there is also an aura of mystery, when she seduces us with the fiery gestures, rapid-fire thoughts and scattered emotions of her Sagittarius Sun and Moon. In contrast, with his Fixed Leo Moon, Eastwood has a well anchored public mask.

Even with the Cardinal Air of his **LIBRA Sun**, *Mark Harmon* sees his world through the lens of his Scorpio Ascendant. With all the crime and mayhem, his CSI world is far more disturbing, than most of us want to believe.

With Scorpio rising, Spring-born **ARIES** *James Franco*'s Sun is near his Descendant. With this (and a Virgo Moon), Franco believes that "service to others is the key to happiness". Yes, Scorpio Rising Signs can also be nice.

"*Ghost Whisperer*" *Jennifer Love Hewitt's* **Scorpio Rising** reveals the secret world of bygone spirits. With her **PISCES Sun**, these insights are willingly accepted, for she is able to make them less frightening.

With **TAURUS** *Janet Jackson*, her Sun and Ascendant are both in the Mode of Fixity. This reinforces this modal quality. What we see are the wide, flat cheek bones and high forehead of Scorpio, and the eyes that are half bovine—and half eagle!

Sagittarius Ascendants

As the darkest day of the year nears, there is still plenty of light to see the path ahead, as the Centaur gallops toward the finish line in the year.

The Fixed Fire of **LEO** *Sean Penn*'s Sun is constantly redirected, as his Archer Ascendant shoots arrows in multiple directions. These fiery arrows light up an array of different paths for him to pursue.

With **AQUARIUS** *Ellen DeGeneras* , the shocking antics of her rebellious Sun are hard to contain. When an idea pops into her head, it is rarely held back by her painfully blunt Centaur Ascendant. With her Aries Moon, it happens instantly.

In the passive Sun Signs, the expansive impulses are more restrained.

CAPRICORN *Bradley Cooper*'s front gate is wide open, and this inspires him to tackle any task and charge up any mountain. This tenacious goat writes, directs, produces and performs in most of his entertainment works.

VIRGO *Pink* (Alecia Beth Moore) has a Mutable Sun and Ascendant. They enhance the screwed features and height of her face. With a fiery Aries Moon, nothing stops this lady from getting what she wants.

The large pupilage in **SCORPIO** *Ann Hathaway*'s eyes show the depth of her Fixed Water Sun. However, her long neck, skewed chin and pointed ears and cheerful smile are products of her Centaur Ascendant.

With his long face, angled chin and wide smile, few would guess *Stephen Colbert* to be a **TAURUS Sun**. Jupiter, his Ascendant's ruler forms the most aspects in his chart—and he has a Gemini Moon! That explains his gift for comedy and improvisation.

Capricorn Ascendants

When the Sun rises in the Sign of Capricorn, a new cycle of time begins, to start another day, and another year of creation! Through this Capricorn window, the course of current and future events is clearly seen, since every moment brings a new goal and another mountain to climb.

The underlying bone structure of **LIBRA** *Susan Sarrandon* shows the granite features of a goat. Note how her double Cardinal placements push her facial features sideways and upward, to create her large head. She also shows the large upper lip plate, that is seen in most Capricorns.

AQUARIUS *Tom Selleck*'s shows the wide-set cheek bones and eyes— and also the bushy brows of Capricorn. His whole face appears to be anchored in granite, when his Fixed Air Sun is not radiating its light.

TAURUS *Bono* and **VIRGO** *Sean Connery* both show the broad sunken cheekbones and down-turned snout of the goat. Bono's face is quite long for a Taurus, for his earthy Sun and Ascendant are both in the Virgo decan. That makes his features similar to that we see in Virgo Connery.

Fire Signs *LEO Lucille Ball* and **SAGITTARIUS** *Jane Fonda* show little of the physical structure of their earthy Ascendant (save for the wide chin and flat cheekbones). However, they show us how the drive of a Cardinal Earth Ascendant keeps one on course, to succeed in any business.

Lucy's success led to the creation of *Desilu studios*—one of the biggest production companies in the early days of television. As for Fonda, she created an empire, by using the athletic adeptness of her Archer Sun, to teach others how to become physically fit.

Aquarius Ascendants

In the month of Aquarius, the radiating beams of dawn's light are growing brighter everyday. This instills hope in the moment of the now, and in all-of-the-future that lies ahead.

With **GEMINI** *Michael J. Fox and* **VIRGO** *Amy Poehler,* the lines of their Mutable Suns are locked into the shield of their Fixed Air Ascendants. This pulls their facial elements tightly together into the center of the face—as it forms their tightly drawn smiles. Their faces have the cubical features of Fixity, but they are also slightly skewed.

The **Fixed Earth** of *Jay Leno*'s **TAURUS SUN** is enhanced by his **Fixed Air Ascendant**. This gives him a larger than normal head, compacted facial components and a large jaw. Likely, it is Jupiter's tight conjunction to his Ascendant and its snug trine to Uranus, that contributes to his odd facial features; Positively, this Jupiter and Uranus also gave him the quick wit, that made him a legend in late night television.

With the "double fixity" of **LEO** *J.K. Rowlings*' luminaries, the square features of the Lion are strong, but her face is not as compacted as we see in Jay Leno. This is likely because of her expansive Sun, and her five components in **Mutable Virgo**. [Virgo explains her mastery of words].

The heads of the Cardinal Signs **LIBRA** *Matt Damon* and **CANCER** *Cyndi Lauper* appear to be squeezed inward from the sides, rather than from the top and bottom. This sideways contraction pulls the eyelids down on the outer edges, and this creates Aquarius' most identifiable trait.

Pisces Ascendants

When Pisces rises in the morning light, it is clear that the cycle of winter is coming to an end. In this twilight before Spring, there is a feeling that a rebirth of life is about to occur. This joyous feeling permeates all things.

When the Mutable Suns of **SAGITTARIUS** *Billi Elish* and **GEMINI** *Laura Dern* are inundated in the Mutable Water of Pisces, their faces balloon and round, as their eyes turn into pools of shimmering light.

With **LIBRA** *Gwyneth Paltrow*, the stirring waters of Pisces seem to do little to disrupt the serenity that she exhibits in her Venus-ruled Sun. Physically, the most notable change is the enlarged pupil in her right eye. Naturally, it peers off in the opposite direction than the other.

Like Paltrow, **TAURUS** *George Clooney* also has a Venus-ruled Sun and that delightful Pisces look in his eyes. However, with this earthy Sun and Capricorn Moon, his emotions are firmly anchored on the ocean's floor.

In **CANCER** *Ringo Starr*, the swirling waters of his Pisces Ascendant are pulled in opposite directions by the Cardinal Water of his Sun. Entangled in the netting of his Pisces mask, both sides of his face mirror each other —as they point in opposite portal directions!

SCORPIO *Ryan Gosling* shows the high forehead and flat cheekbones of his Fixed Sun. However, he lacks Scorpio's large eyes, and his facial features are pinched together into the center of his face. This Aquarius trait may be due to his Sun's conjunction to Aquarius' ruling planet Uranus—and their trine to his highly malleable Pisces Ascendant.

With this definition of traits, we now go to a deeper level of definition with the Decans of the Signs.

Decans of the Zodiac Signs

In time, astrologers recognized the physical features of their Sun Signs were not consistent. With this, they recognized that there was a "Trinity of Modal Patterns" operating within each of the **10°** within each **30°** Sign. These degrees (or decans) unfold in the sequential order of the three Sign's within the parent element. Here, we show how the three decans in each of the Elements alters one's appearance.

The *First Decan* (**1°** to **9°**) delivers the Mode of the Sign of placement. The *Second Decan* (**10°** to **19°**) injects the qualities of the next Mode in the Element. The *Third Decan* (**20°** to **30°**) displays the traits of the final Mode in the parent Element. This concept is easily observed in the bone structure of the Ascendant and Sun. The Moon is less obvious.

Let's start with decans of the Fire Signs.
Aries Sun Signs:

With *Leonard Nimoy's* **4°Aries Sun** (1st decan), the **Cardinal Fires** are initiated, as his Sun's placement in this decan gives him strong Ram features. Other chart components make Nimoy appear less forceful, but the long and convex facial traits of Aries are obvious.

Cardinality is followed by Fixity—thusly the **2nd decan** of **Aries** takes us to the next Fire Sign: **Fixed Leo**.

Robert Downey's **14° Leo Sun** still displays the forceful qualities of the Ram, but his fires are more contained. This decan shortens the face, as it squares the snout and jaw—to form traits that hint of the Leo Lion.

Conan O'Brien's abrupt Ram energies are dispersed by his **28°** Sun's placement in the **Mutable** or **3rd decan** of **Aries: Sagittarius**. Here, the Centaur's playful fires give this Ram his animated gestures and a boundless sense of comedy. This Mutable decan twists and offsets the long facial features of his Sun.

Leo Sun Signs:

Jerry Garcia has a **9°** Leo Sun. In this **1st decan of Leo**, the Fixed magnetic stage presence and the purring confidence of **Leo** radiates outward. With Jerry, the abundant hair of his Lion mane adds to the show.

Barrack Obama's **13° Leo Sun** is in the **2nd decan** of **Leo**. Since **Sagittarius** is the next Fire Sign in the circle, this lion's typically cubical features are long and skewed. The unflappable confidence of the Lion remains, but the Mutable Fire is also there. This gives his Sun the cheerful, optimistic and philosophical insights of the Centaur.

Sean Penn's **27° Leo Sun** makes him a resident of the **Cardinal decan** of Leo—**Aries**. Of the three lions, Sean is the most forceful in expressing his personal opinions. With his angular forehead and convex facial lines, he also hints of the features of a Ram.

Sagittarius Sun Signs:

Bette Midler's **9°** Sun places her in the **1st decan** of **Mutable Sagittarius**. This takes her down the winding road, where galloping horses freely run. Along with

◆Aries	◆Leo	◆Sagittarius

her sense of humor and animated gestures, we see the eyes, bulbous nose and extended jaw of the horse.

Teri Hatcher's **16°** Sun places her in the **Cardinal** or **Aries decan** of **Sagittarius**. Of the three, she is the most directed and often the first to charge head-first into action. The long Centaur face remains, but the convex structure of the face suggests features of the Ram.

With *Jane Fonda's* **29°** Sun, the **Fixed decan of Leo** quells the galloping energies, as it gives her Leo's facial features and sense of showmanship. This fixing of her athletic Sun helped her to gain fame as an exercise instructor.

Air Sign Decans

The three decans give each of the Air Signs their own set of modal variances. This alters the pattern and manner in which their mental natures are expressed.

Gemini Sun Signs:

With his mercuric gift with words, **Bob Dylan** stirred the minds of a generation with his force of **Mutable Air**. His **3° 1st decan Sun** shows the billowing whirls of hair, the offset eyes and brows and the curved, down-turned nose—all typical traits of Gemini.

Marilyn Monroe's **10° Sun** places her in the **2nd** or **Libra decan** of Gemini. Libra added Venus' beauty and attractiveness—but these Cardinal forces kept her mind in a constant whirl. With an Aquarius Moon trine her Sun, true romance was hard for her to find.

Paula Abdul's **28°** Sun is in the **3rd** or **Aquarius decan** of Gemini. With her cubical skull. rectangular jaw structure and her tight-lipped smile, Paula displays many of the physical traits of Aquarius.

Her expression shows how the cognitive connections in the mercuric mind of Gemini can be locked into some alternate reality.

Libra Sun Signs:

Gyneth Paltrow, like many acclaimed beauties (i.e., **Bridgett Bardot** and **Cheryl Tiegs**) is a **1st decan Libra**. They all show the well proportioned features, the lovely almond eyes and V-lined smile associated with Libra.

Simon Cowell's **13° Sun** is in the **2nd** or **Aquarius decan** of **Libra**. Simon shows little of the niceties of Libra. What we experience is the intense placement of Mars near his Sun. Physically, he displays hints of the Water Bearer's square skull and jaw and the compacted face of Fixed Air. Note how his eyelids tilt down on the outside, when he focuses his eyes on some distant point. *[To see a triple Libra who looks like an Aquarius, check out Kate Winslet's decans on page 89]*.

Tom Petty's **26° Sun** makes him a resident of the **Gemini decan** of **Libra**. Mercuric Gemini gave this Libra artist the gift for words. They got him inducted into "The Song Writers Hall of Fame".

Aquarius Sun Signs:

Alan Alda's **7° Aquarius Sun** is in the 1st decan. Like all the others, this enhances the qualities of his Sun Sign. This Sun's trine to Mars and square to Uranus made him a revolutionary spokesman for humanitarian and anti--war causes. Physically, he shows the large cubical skull,

◆Gemini　　◆Libra　　◆Aquarius

the dimpled cheeks, the compacted eyes and the tight lipped, down-drawn mouth of Aquarius.

Chris Rock's **18° Sun** is in the **2nd decan.** In this shift into the Air Sign that follows Aquarius in the wheel. Chris shows the Mutable energies of **Gemini**.

Of the three Aquarians pictured here, he is the most mercuric of the group. His intuitive "sense of the outrageous" is communicated at a rapid pace, as his mind jumps from one thought to another. With his rapid blinks, his offset eyes and the long offset chin, he gives us hints of Gemini's physical traits.

Jennifer Annison's **23° Sun** is placed in **Libra's 3rd decan.** Jenny's cool solar energies are warmed by the easy going charm and smile of Libra. This Cardinal Air gives her Fixed Sun direction and balance. However, underneath the tranquil surface, the impulsive Aquarian urges are stirring. Any second, you can expect the release of some unexpected surprises.

Earth Sign Decans

All **Earth Sign Suns** display earthy solar traits, but with the Sun's placement in different decans, the quality of that Earth is altered in a manner that is indicative of the next Earth Sign, that follows the order in the Zodiac wheel.

◆**Taurus**　　◆**Virgo**　　◆**Capricorn**

Taurus Sun Signs:

Jessica Lange's Sun, in the **1st decan** of **Taurus**, captures the initial solidifying moments of **Fixed Earth**. Jessica shows the square jaw and skull, the broad flat eyebrows and the full pupilage of her bovine eyes. She is the most anchored of the three.

Audrey Hepburn's **13°** (2nd decan) **Sun** places her in the **Virgo decan** of **Taurus**. Her Taurus sensuality seems to be delicately mixed with Virgo's Mutable forces. She shows the lanky body, the long "Bambi face and neck" and the meticulously proper personality of the Virgin.

Cate Blancett's **27°** Sun makes her a resident of the **Capricorn decan** of **Taurus**. The lusty sensuality of Taurus remains, but she seems cooler and paler. Also, the wide high-set cheek bones suggest qualities of the Cardinal driven goat. Often, Cate's steely eyes seem to be focused on the foliage, on distant mountain tops

Virgo Sun Signs:

Of all of the individuals in this collection, *Lily Tomlin* is the quintessential Virgo. With her **7° Sun**, the nervous, mercuric and fussy energies are accented, as she displays the long face and nose, the puckered lips and the twisted features of Mutable Earth.

Jane Curtin's **13° Sun** places her in **Virgo's 2nd decan**. Here we see traits of the Earth Sign that follows Virgo—**Capricorn**! The features of the goat are mixed in with those of her Sun. Jane projects Virgo's nitpicking critical-ness and also the sarcastic cynicism and pushy qualities of the sea goat.

Bill Murray's **27° Sun** places him in the **3rd** or **Taurus decan** of **Virgo**. With Taurus' fixity, he appears less adaptable than the average Virgo. His characters often seem immobilized by their excessive worrying—'cuz they're unable to let go of anything!

Murray displays the cubical skull, the boxlike jaw and chin and the square features of Fixity. His eyes appear more relaxed than what we see in the typical Virgo.

Capricorn Sun Signs:

Anthony Hopkins **9° Capricorn Sun** makes the cold, hard-driven Cardinality of his Sun obvious. Physically, he shows the chiselled features, high forehead and the beady eyes that sit high under his bushy brows. The depressions between his wide-set cheekbones makes him appear solemn and serious.

Mel Gibson's **12° Sun** is in the **2nd** *or* **Taurus** decan of Capricorn. This makes his body stockier, most noticeably in the shoulders. The square forehead, jaw and chin are what we see in Fixed Earth.

Oddly, Mel's Capricorn Sun, Libra Moon and Cancer Ascendant are all in Cardinal Signs. It may be his 5 planets in Fixed Signs that add to his Fixed Nature.

Kevin Costner's **28 degree Sun** injects **Virgo's** Mercury into his Capricorn veins. With this **3rd decan Capricorn Sun** (and his Virgo Ascendant), Kevin is the most mercuric and analytical of these three goats. This gives him the long, twisted face, the wide mouth and the offset, squinted eyes that are associated with Virgo.

Water Sign Decans

Within each decan of the Water Signs, the liquid oceans surge, settle and churn, as the wheel of time changes degree by degree. These differences in degree alter the emotional nature of the Water Signs.

Cancer Sun Signs:

Ross Perot is a 1st decan Cancer Sun with a 1st decan Cancer Rising. With this double-decan, the round "Full-Moon face" of the crab becomes obvious.

With her **12° Sun** and **11° Ascendant** both in the **2nd Scorpio decan** of **Cancer**, *Leona Helmsley* displays a combination of Cancer and Scorpio's physical features. This also made her cruel and unforgiving. With this Scorpio, she became known as the "Queen of Mean".

Phoebe Snow's **24° Sun** and **24° Ascendant** are both in the **3rd** or **Pisces decan** of **Cancer.** This dreamy Crab often escaped into her fantasy world of music. It made the world more delightful for all of us.

On page 77, we show how this Scorpio decan helps us to identify Cancer Tom Cruise's unknown Ascendant.

Scorpio Sun Signs:

First decan Scorpio *Burt Lancaster* shows many of the traits of Fixed Water, notably the square forehead, the flat cheeks and the large beak. Burt was a legendary movie star whose integrity remained solid throughout his career. In his long career, he showed us that fixed emotions aren't subject to changing social trends and whims.

With his **16° Scorpio Sun** in the **Pisces decan**, *Carl Sagan* was a true star gazer, whose connection to the universe was more than he imagined. This decan gave him the offset brows and chin, and the dreamy eyes of Pisces. With stubborn Taurus Rising, Carl constantly criticized astrology and he refused to study the valuable lessons of this ancient art.

Whoppi Goldberg's **20°** Sun resides in **the 3rd** or **Cancer** decan of **Scorpio**. This position adds movement to the Fixed nature of her Sun, for it gives her the drive to emphatically state her opinions! In the process, we see the swelled Full-Moon temples of the crab.

Pisces Sun Signs:

Drew Barrymore's **3° Sun** makes her a **1st decan Pisces**. With her large dreamy fish eyes, joyous sense of fantasy and her bubbly and constantly shifting facial expressions, Drew shows the quintessential energies of Mutable Water.

With a **10° Pisces Sun**, *Ron Howard*'s imagination is directed by the tidal Cardinal forces of his **Cancer decan Sun**. This push is also driven by his Cardinal Aries Moon and Capricorn Ascendant. This drive made him the highly successful producer and director of many delightful movies. His Aries Ascendant gives his face greater height, but he still shows the round temples of the Cancer crab.

Glenn Close's **28° Sun** is in the **Scorpio decan** of **Pisces**. This lady's incredibly intense and seductive emotions are not what we'd expect from a Pisces. Also, with her Moon and Ascendant in Fixed Signs, Glenn's emotions appear to be always in control.

The Decans Work Everywhere!

These triad divisions in each Sign apply to both luminaries and also the planets. However, these decan variances are most easily seen in the bone structure of one's Ascendant. This can help to pinpoint the degree of a person's missing Ascendant.

The Effects of Planetary Aspects & Placements

In this book's opening, we showed the *five angles* in the *Sacred Solids* and how the ancients believed them to be the shaping forces of all physical structures. Shortly after, we noted how *the angle of the Equator* i.e., shaped one's Sun Sign, Moon and Ascendant features. Here, we show how the **angles (i.e., aspects)** of the personal planets can alter the shape and/or quality of a person's Sun, Moon or Rising Sign.

The Personal Planets alter the natures of one's Sun and Moon Sign

A planet's placement in a Sign changes its nature

The upper photos show the mercuric, electrical and airy expressions of **Gene Wilder's Gemini Ascendant** and **Sun**. The lower photo shows what happens when Gene makes his initial contacts and conversations with others. Both of their natures are altered by the placement of his **Venus** and **Mercury**.

When Gene attempts to connect to others, he becomes surprisingly sly and protective. If he is feeling uncomfortable and conversation arises— the chatter ceases and he becomes emotional. His personal planets Venus and Mercury are in the **Water Sign** of **Cancer**.

When these two personal planets are activated, watch how his facial flesh swells, as his pupils enlarge into pools of water. It reminds us of the mannerisms of the Cancer crab.

Gene Wilder: 6/11/1933. 3:50 A.M., Milwaukee, WI.

How a **Cancer Moon** changes the appearance of one's Sun

Because of Cancer's rulership of the Moon, most **Sun Signs with Cancer Moons** show the saturated flesh and round lunar temples of the crab, even when they are not reflecting the emotions of their Cancer Moons.

Tom Watts, Heath Ledger and Nicole Richie have Cancer Moons.

MARS on the Ascendant brings incredible athletic skills

Joe Dimaggio
11/25/1914,
7:00 AM
Martinez, CA

Joe Dimaggio's **Sun, Mars** and **Ascendant** are all conjoined in Sagittarius.

This baseball legend's **Mars** also sextiles **Jupiter**, the ruler of his Sagittarius Sun. This gave Joe a wide range of athletic skills. With this, he became known as the best all-around player in the history of the game.

Statisticians *Michel & Francoise Gauquelin's* studies of birth charts found that large numbers of eminent athletes and sports champions had the planet Mars conjoined their Ascendant or near their Midheaven.

See page 30, we showed how to recognize the Mars of individuals, by observing the force and patterns of their movements, when they are performing a physical task.

Pluto's trine to the Sun brings Strength & Power

Olympic swimmer **Michael Phelps** is a **Cancer Sun***, yet he shows little of the round, lunar features of the crab. With **Mars** conjoined his Sun and Ascendant, he has the long face associated with **Aries**, the Sign that is ruled by *Mars*.

The Fixed intensity in Michael's eyes can be attributed to his Sun's trine to **Pluto**. This outer planet is the ruler of **Scorpio**.

Michael Phelps: 6/30/1985 Baltimore, MD
*Unvaried time also gives him **Cancer Rising**

Examples on the impact of the personal planets on the personalties of other celebrities can be seen in the 24 *Celebrity Snapshots* that begin on page 84.

Next, let's look at the OUTER PLANETS and show how their aspects alter a person's physical traits.

76

Aspects of the Outer Planets create powerful changes

JUPITER bring giant exaggerations

Jupiter is the largest planet and appropriately its role is to expand and enlarge everything that it contacts.

Leno's Jupiter is at 20° Pisces. It conjoins his **Aquarius Ascendant** and squares his **Taurus Sun**. Since the *lower jaw and chin are ruled by Taurus*, and the Rising Sign defines one's bone structure, this aspect likely accounts for Leno's large and highly exaggerated jaw.

In addition, Jupiter also trines his Uranus, the ruler of his Ascendant. Not only is his jaw large, it is also highly distorted.

4/28/1950, 2:03 AM, Rochelle (NY)

Saturn on the Midheaven

The Duke **John Wayne** have his Sun, ASC and Mercury conjoined in the Mutable Air Sign of **Gemini.** This did not fit his slow-talking and lumbering mannerisms. This may be due to Uranus' conjunction to his Capricorn Mars and their sextile to his secretive Scorpio Moon. With Saturn in his 10th House, his rock-solid image brought him much success.

May 26, 1907, 5:00 AM / Winterset (IA)

NEPTUNE waters the imagination

Billie Ellish's **Aquarius Moon** is conjoined by **Neptune**, the ruler of her **Pisces Ascendant**. This Rising Sign trines **Jupiter,** the ruler of her **Sagittarius Sun**, while **Uranus** (the ruler of her **Aquarius Moon**) sextiles her **Sun**. Also, her Rising Sign squares **Saturn** and **Pluto** —and Pluto sextiles her Moon and Uranus. Her solar light, lunar emotions and physical shield seem inseparable.

Saturn constructs the dreamy "Ocean Eyes" of the Pisces Fish, while Pluto's sextile to her Moon and Uranus creates her other-worldly and emotionally distanced persona.

12/18/2001,11:30 AM, Los Angeles, CA

Mars, Neptune & Uranus bring a diverse range of talents

Bradley Cooper's demeanor is one of strength, machismo and tenacity. In 2014, he won his first Oscar, producing the action drama *"American Sniper".* Mars' conjunction on his **Centaur Ascendant** gives him this tough martial appearance.

Four years later, the genre changed from action to romance, when Bradley starred in and directed *A Star is Born.* Cooper's gift of music is a product of Neptune's conjunction to Mars and his Rising Sign. Mars sextile to his **Libra Moon** (and its conjunction to Uranus) gives him his strong verbal skills.

With a **Capricorn Sun** and all of his planets on the left side of his chart, he is highly driven to make it to the top of any mountain. As of 2021, he had been nominated for 8 Academy and Tony Awards, and won two Grammies and a BAFTA trophy for his film *Silver Linings Playbook.*

1/5/1997, 5:09 A.M., Philadelphia, PA

Jupiter, Saturn, Neptune, Uranus & Pluto bring a giant array of surprises

When all five outer planets were aspected to the key lights in the sky, it gave Hollywood one of its "most unusual character actors".

Few would expect **Steve Buscemi** to have a **Sagittarius Sun**. Why, you ask? Saturn conjoins his Sun and squares his **Virgo Moon** and **Pisces Ascendant**. Also, **Jupiter**— his Sun's ruler—conjoins **Neptune** and this dreamy planet also squares **Uranus** and sextiles **Pluto**. Together, they explain this Centaur's outrageously macabre sense of comedy.

With these outer planet aspects to Pluto, Steve became known for "finding his demise" in most of his roles. With his likely Pisces Ascendant, he has a gift for enlisting sympathy from others, as he encounters his array of reoccurring tribulations.

(12/13/1957 11:30 A.M.(?) Brooklyn, NY

How to Guess a Person's Unknown Ascendant

Actor **Tom Cruise**'s Ascendant is uncertain. *Lois Rodden* claimed he was **Gemini Rising**. *Dell Horoscope Magazine* declared him to be **Virgo Rising**. *Astrotheme, Astrodienst* and *others* found consensus in a birth time of 3:15 P.M.; It gave him a **Scorpio Ascendant**. Here, we will explain how physical traits can help us to determine Tom Cruise's Ascendant. Surprisingly, this author contents it is not one of those above.

FIRST STEP—Run your subject's chart:
We know Tom was born on July 3, 1962, in Syracuse, NY. So *the first thing we did* was to print a chart **for sunrise on that date**. It was at 5:30 A.M. *[Google tells you the time of Sunrise on any date, at any location.]* This places his Sun on the eastern horizon.

SECOND STEP—Capture images of your subject:

Watch your subject and gather images *(in your mind and in photos)*. Find **moments of neutral expression**, when your subject is NOT showing the projections of his/her Sun, or the reactions of the Moon. Here, with Tom's **Sun** at **11º Cancer**, we know that his "bone structure and features" should resemble those of *Leona Helmsley*, a person with her Sun and Ascendent in the **2nd Decan of Cancer**. As noted on page 70, this decan is a combo of Cancer and Scorpio traits. Any variances are likely due to a different Ascendant.

Next, spin the chart, to find feasible Rising Signs—that may instill physical features, that are different than what we see in a 2nd decan Cancer Sun. Also consider impact of other planets, particularly any, that may conjoins one of his luminaries.

Tom's left pic gives hints of a 2nd decan Cancer. It shows the round lunar temples of Cancer, as well as the high forehead, bushy brows and the flat, down-drawn cheek bones of **Scorpio**. The right photo tells us that Tom's Ascendant needs to make his Cancer face longer in height, eliminate the lunar temples and create a higher forehead. Notably, all three pictures suggest a strong presence of Fixity. Since Leo Rising places his Uranus and Pluto in his 1st House, Leo may be a possible Rising Sign—since Uranus on the Ascendant would for the inward pull of his eyelids.

THIRD STEP—Study the Chart, to Narrow Ascendant Choices:

With his high public profile and driven nature, Cruise should have strong components in the left and upper half of his chart. With his success in action films, Neptune and Mars should be in powerful positions—perhaps near one of the cross points in his chart. With Cruise's cubical bone structure and close-set eyes it is likely his Ascendant is not a Cardinal or Mutable Sign.

Tom's Moon is in Cancer until 9:55 A.M., *then it moves into **Leo***. We know that, with the Moon's rulership of Cancer, a Cancer Moon greatly affects the physical appearance of all Sun Signs. Oddly, even with a Cancer Sun, Tom shows few features of a crab. He lacks the large pupillage often seen in Water Signs and he rarely shows the timid mannerisms of a Cancer Sun or Moon. *Therefore, it is likely his **Moon is in Leo**!*

When Tom's Moon goes into Leo, **2° Virgo** is rising. Thusly, his Ascendant will be one of the *Signs between Virgo and 21° Pisces (the Sign Rising at the end of his day of birth)*. With this, *the previous Signs of Cancer, Gemini, Taurus, Aries and Pisces are eliminated*. **All Signs between Leo and Aquarius are possible.** Those who claim him to be **Scorpio Rising** give him a birth time of 3:00 P.M. Here, Uranus and Pluto are in his 10th House and Neptune is on his Ascendant, but his 7th House Mars is not in a strong position.

Dell Horoscope's 12:05 P.M. chart gives Tom a *Taurus decan* of **Virgo** Rising. This Taurus decan would account for Tom's large neck and stocky features—but he displays little of the mercuric qualities of Virgo, or the skewed features of Mutable Earth. With that, we believe Tom does NOT have **Virgo Rising.**

The best method for guessing an Ascendant is to *"Watch the body language of your subjects, when they enter a room!"*. Here, they are unknowingly making their "1st impression" of their Ascendant, as they present themselves to others. Do they move in unhesitatingly, or passively? That usually tells us if they have a Masculine or Feminine Ascendant. When Tom enters "a scene", the first impression that we see of is not hesitant, but distinctly unabated. *His Ascendant is likely masculine.*

Tom's face lacks the wide-mouth and horizontal spread eyes of Libra—and charm and pleasantry are not part of his public persona. Therefore, Tom's (2:30 P.M.) Ascendant is likely not **Libra.** However, his distance demeanor may be due to Uranus' conjunction to Venus—or perhaps him being **Aquarius Rising** (10 P.M.). Notably, this Rising Sign places Tom's four components in Libra's 7th House, and the 8:30 P.M. time for **Capricorn Rising**, places his Moon, Sun and Venus in the 7th House. This eliminates 3 Rising Signs!

With a Leo Moon, a **Sagittarius Ascendant** would make Tom a "double fire". In his role in *"Risky Business"*, he showed little of the fiery and Mutable gestures of Sagittarius. The only Sign left—that places Mars and Uranus near one of the cross points—is **Leo Rising! That is our choice for his Ascendant!**

FOURTH STEP: Find Images of Identical Suns and Ascendants

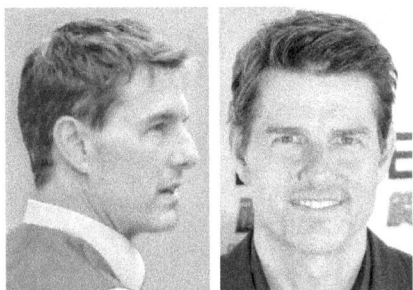

Tom's left-upper photo displays the cubical head of the Lion. It's what we would expect from someone with a cluster of Leo planets near a Leo Ascendant. To confirm our choice, this author searched through *Astrotheme*'s list of charts and found six individuals who share the same decan of Tom's Sun, and our chosen Rising Sign. The closest was French politician *Vincent Peillon*, who was born two years before Cruise.

Peillon's Moon is in Sagittarius, in the decan of Leo. Uranus and Pluto also conjunct his Ascendant. This match on components shows why both share similar physical features. Other **Cancer Suns** with **Leo Risings** (in the same decan) are *Toby Maguire, George Bush* and *Richard Branson*.

Yes, it gets complicated—but hopefully, these two pages have given the reader a few methods on how to use physical traits to identify a person's Ascendant. Of course, the final confirmation comes from the rectifications of the events in a person's life—for the Ascendant is the starting point, where all of the events in a person's life unfold.

July 7, 1960 / 9:00 A.M., Suresnes, France

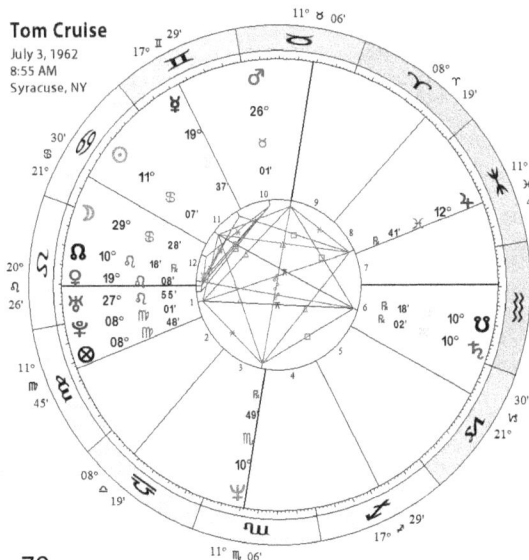

Tom Cruise
July 3, 1962
8:55 AM
Syracuse, NY

This method for identifying Rising Signs evolved from this author's collaboration with Astrologer *Marc Penfield*, who asked me to "use physical traits" to help him identify the unknown Rising Signs of several celebrities (including Cruise). Marc's rectification of events in Tom's life, supported this author's contention *that Tom Cruise has Leo Rising!*

Still *Astrotheme* and *Astrodienst* list Tom as **Scorpio Rising**, and their sources also found transits to support their choice. This is why finding an "unknown Ascendant" is so difficult. However, it becomes a little easier—when you follow the physical clues!

79

How the Eyes are Altered by Aspects to the Sun & Moon

For many years, Vedic astrologers have decreed that the masculine **Sun** governs the **right eye** and the feminine **Moon** rules the **left eye.** This may be why the Right Eye is dominate in males, and the Left Eye reigns in females. Some claim that afflictions in the **Right Eye** are caused by hard aspects in the **2nd House,** and it is in the **12th House** for the **Left Eye.**

Here, to show whether this *Sun-ruled RIGHT EYE* and *Moon-ruled LEFT EYE* concept has validity, this book will look at six subjects with unusual eye features. Amazingly, it is the aspects of *expansive Jupiter* and *constrictive Saturn* that reflect the irregularities in their face divisions.

This concept of facial division is supported in psychologist Julian Jaynes' 1976 book on the **bicameral mind.** In it, he claims that methodical people are *left-brained* and their left brain operates *the right side of the body.* In opposition, artistic people are *right-brain* oriented and it operates *the left side of the body.*

Subjects with dominant Left Eyes:

The three men on the left all appear to have enlarged left eyes. This contradicts the belief that the RIGHT EYE dominates in males. These aberrations are likely due to the Jupiter and Saturn aspects to their Suns and Moons.

Jeff Bezos' Capricorn Sun squares his Aries Ascendant—and his Rising Sign conjoins Jupiter and trines his Sagittarius Moon. These Jupiter aspects tell us why his Moon-Ruled LEFT Eye is larger.

Billy Joel's Taurus Sun conjoins its ruler Venus. Saturn's square to his Venus makes his *Sun-Ruled Right Eye* smaller. All the while, Jupiter's trine to his **Libra Moon** makes his *Moon-Ruled Left Eye* larger. Meanwhile, his "dreamy Pisces look" can be attributed to Neptune's conjunction to his Moon.

Subjects with dominant Right Eyes:

The right eyes of **Maya Angelou** and character actress **Tracee Ellis Ross** are extra large. This contradicts the premise that the Left Eye dominates in females. Like with the three men, this irregularity is a product of the aspects of Saturn and Jupiter to their Suns and Moons.

Respectively, both ladies have **Jupiter** conjoining and sextiling their *Right-Eyed Ruled Suns.* This makes their right eyes noticeably larger than their left eyes. All the while, Maya's and Tracee's Moons both sextile **Saturn** and this makes their *Moon-Ruled Left Eyes* smaller. Tracee's trine of Saturn

See more on Eye shapes, on page 31

to Uranus likely accounts for her abnormally out-of-proportion eyes. It may have been her Saturn's placement in her *2nd House,* that brought on this affliction in her right eye.

Here, Jupiter and Saturn's effects are reversed—Uranus is in Control

Like the two previous ladies, **Tina Fey**'s *Sun-Ruled Right Eye* is the largest, and like Bezos, one side of her face is larger than the other. What is odd here is that Fey's right eye is much larger—even though Jupiter is conjoining her Left-Eye ruling. This appearance is partly due to her right face's larger bone structure, a product of her Jupiter's square and Uranus' sextile to her **Leo Ascendant.** This irregularity is enhanced by her Moon's conjunction and Jupiter's trine to Venus—the planet that rules her **Taurus Sun** and **Libra Moon.** Whether she's projecting her Sun or her Moon, the Right Eye remains dominant.

Marty Feldman's Jupiter trines his *Right-Eye Ruled* **Cancer Sun.** Since his left eye is far larger, the Jupiter effect is wrong again. This is likely due to Uranus' square to his Moon. Since his Ascendant is unknown, the balanced facial bone structure suggests that his Ascendant makes no aspects to Jupiter or Saturn.

*This short list of "odd-eyed celebrities" needs a larger sample to verify these observations. This author suggests that readers check out the charts of **Jane Seymore, Sly Stallone, Peter Falk** and **Buster Keaton,** to see whether their charts contain the Sun/Moon and various Jupiter, Saturn and/or Uranus aspects that were examined here.*

In their keen observances of the cycles of time, astrologers also discovered that individuals would appear *to age in a manner* that suggested that their chart components were progressing **One Degree** *for Every Year in their lives*. With their Sun's progression, they saw a evolving sense of "Self", while their Moon's altered their emotions, etc. Here, we show how one's progressed Sun and Moon alter one's physical appearance, and also predict the events in a person's life.

Time Changes Everything
Paul McCartney
6/18/1942, 2:00 P.M. Liverpool, UK
Sun: 26°37′ **Gemini** / ASC: 25°18′ Virgo
Moon: 17°26′ **Leo**

The Sun's Progression into a New Sign brings Creative and Physical Changes

At the age of 5, Paul's Gemini Sun progressed into <u>Cancer</u>.

*Note: The left picture above shows how the original force of McCartney's Sun remains throughout their life. It was this **Mutable Air** of **Paul MCartney**'s **Gemini Sun** that made him part of the greatest lyric composing team of his time.*

In his fifth year of life (1947), Paul's **26°** Gemini Sun progressed into Cancer. This softened the flighty nature of his mercuric Sun. It also physically inflated his flesh, to gave us hints of the physical traits and manners of a Crab.

With his bass guitar and keyboard skills--and the progressed Cardinal Waters of his Sun—Paul's rhythmic contributions kept the other *Beatles* musically in sync with each other. Two+ decades later, Paul was feeling his Sun's future progression into Leo, as well as his desire to become "the leader of the Band". In 1971, he left *The Beatles* to form the band *Wings*. In 1978, at age 36, he escaped to his farm in Scotland with his wife Linda. Bigger changes were just ahead!

At the age of 35, Paul's Sun progressed into <u>Leo</u>.

In 1977, when his **Sun progressed into Leo**, Paul begin his grandiose creative binge! In the next three decades, Leo's reign inspired Paul to master his showmanship in an diverse array of musical creations. He produced a series of solo albums, created the movie *Give My Regards to Broad Street* and began his 1991 commission for Liverpool's Philharmonic Society. In this 30 year period, Paul's creative fires also inspired him to create the experimental *Electric Arguments* and his dance score for the New York City Ballet.

In the top photos, the third image shows how the progression of Paul's Sun from Cancer into Leo transformed his facial features. There, the excessive hair and mane of a lion appears, as Paul's features became more Fixed and cubical. The lower photos of a young and older McCartney also show how his Progressed Sun transformed the round features of his Cancer face into those of a Lion.

At the age of 65, Paul's Sun progressed into <u>Virgo</u>.

In 2007, Paul's **Sun** *progressed* into **Virgo**. The 4th photo (in the upper group) shows how his face became longer and how the skewed lines of Mutability became obvious. In this final phase in his life, Paul began the task of serving others by raising billions in his charity concerts, to fund PETA, Food Pantries, Green Peace and other world projects.

Progressions Create Major Life Events

The Sun, Moon, Ascendant and planets all follow the **1° per Year Progression**. With their different lengths of **360° orbits**, the *"time span of each component"* changes Signs and Houses at different rates. Of all of these, the Moon's 28 to 30 day orbital cycle is the shortest. Therefore, it often triggers major events in a person's life. So it was with Paul.

When Paul met Linda Eastman in 1967, his *progressed* **Sun and Moon** were conjoined—and both of them were forming a trine to his *progressed* and *natal* **Venus** in his *progressed 9th House*! Here, Paul found the love of his life and a deeper spiritual purpose. Sadly, in 1998, when Linda lost her battle with Cancer, Paul's *progressed* **Moon** and **Mars** were in his progressed 10th House. Both were squaring his *progressed* **Uranus** and **Saturn** in his progressed **7th House of Marriage**. This gives the reader an idea on how progressions predict changes in a person's life.

This book has only hinted at the predictive effects of progressions, but it has showed how transiting planets at one's birth can predict one's physical appearance. In this book's last chapter on "Celebrity Snapshots", there are many mentions on how the cycles of certain planets (mostly Saturn, Jupiter and Uranus) can also predict the rise and fall in celebrity careers. Since predictive astrology is not the intent of this book, interested readers will need to pursue that subject in other sources.

The Duads add a deeper layer to "The Onion"

The Duad (or Dwadashamsa) provides a deeper division of the wheel! It is used by Hindu astrologers to track long-term family trends—or what could be called "a family's astrological DNA". It reveals "The Dharma" (karma) and growth, that a person will face, in his/her current incarnation.

There are twelve 2.5° Duad divisions in each 30° Zodiac Sign. Starting with any Sign, this division sequences in the order of the Signs to create 144 Duad divisions in the 360° circle. If the subject has an Aries component, the first **Zero to 2.5°** will be known as the *Aries/Aries Duad*. The next **2.5° to 5°** is the *Aries/Taurus Duad*. At **27.5°**, we find the *Aries/Pisces Duad*. This continues through the rest of the Signs. Duads often explain why some people do NOT show the physical traits of their key components. One such person is Jerry Seinfeld.

The 12-Fold Divisions (Duads) in the Signs											
0.0 TO 2.5	2.5 TO 5.0	5.0 TO 7.5	7.5 TO 10	10 TO 12.5	12.5 TO 15	15 TO 17.5	17.5 TO 20	20 TO 22.5	22.5 TO 25	25 TO 27.5	27.5 TO 30
♈	♉	♊	♋	♌	♍	♎	♏	♐	♑	♒	♓
♉	♊	♋	♌	♍	♎	♏	♐	♑	♒	♓	♈
♊	♋	♌	♍	♎	♏	♐	♑	♒	♓	♈	♉
♋	♌	♍	♎	♏	♐	♑	♒	♓	♈	♉	♊
♌	♍	♎	♏	♐	♑	♒	♓	♈	♉	♊	♋
♍	♎	♏	♐	♑	♒	♓	♈	♉	♊	♋	♌
♎	♏	♐	♑	♒	♓	♈	♉	♊	♋	♌	♍
♏	♐	♑	♒	♓	♈	♉	♊	♋	♌	♍	♎
♐	♑	♒	♓	♈	♉	♊	♋	♌	♍	♎	♏
♑	♒	♓	♈	♉	♊	♋	♌	♍	♎	♏	♐
♒	♓	♈	♉	♊	♋	♌	♍	♎	♏	♐	♑
♓	♈	♉	♊	♋	♌	♍	♎	♏	♐	♑	♒

Jerry Seinfeld

4/29/1954, 6 A.M.(?)
Brooklyn, NY
(Birth time not confirmed)

Jerry Seinfeld's **TAURUS Sun** and **Ascendant** explains his lackadaisical manner. Oddly, he shows little of the Fixed mannerisms or cubical features of Taurus. This can be attributed to the Duads in his chart.

Jerry's 6:00 A.M. birth time places his **8° Taurus Sun** in the **Leo Duad**—and it opposes his **5° Saturn** in the **Capricorn Duad** of **Scorpio**. This accounts for Jerry's dry sense of showmanship. This showmanship is given the humor of the Centaur, since, his **18° Taurus Decan Ascendant** is in the **Sagittarius Duad.** Physically, this enhances the angled features of mutability in his face.

The "wishy-washy" nature of this double Taurus can be attributed to his many components in *Water Sign Duads.* The strongest is his **21° Pisces Moon** is in the *Water Duad of Scorpio*. Pisce's ruler **Neptune** is at **24° Libra** (in the *Cancer Duad*) opposing his **28° Mercury** in the *Pisces Duad* of *Aries*. Also, his **24° Jupiter** is in **Gemini** in the *Pisces Duad;* It trines his **Neptune** in **Libra**—in Libra's *Cancer Duad.*

To find your personal Duads, check the chart above!

First, **find the Sign** of one of your key components—as listed in the left "black" vertical column. Next, *follow the horizontal boxes* until it lines up with the "degree of that component." That box will give you the **Duad of that Sign.**

Within the Duads, lie the Sabian Symbols

The Sabian Symbols were created in the 20th Century; They provide ideographic writings on **ALL of the 360 degrees in the Zodiac Wheel.** These symbolic words provide a deeper psychological, emotional and spiritual understanding of the degrees in a person's chart. Their effect on a person's appearance has not yet been explored by this author.

Astrology reveals a Twelve-Step Process of Creation

Previously, this book defined how progressions and the aspects of the personal and distant planets shape the long range patterns in our lives. It is the Decans and Duads that show us how the Signs operate in smaller increments of Time —to program the subtler events in our life.

Next, we show how the 12 Zodiac Signs operate in a grand plan of operation.

DANCE TO THE RHYTHMS
WITH THE 12 STEPS OF CREATION

Now that you know that astrology is a insightful science and also a wonderful art form—it is time to use Nature's repeating cycles (and the movements of all of the objects in the Universe) to help keep your life on its destined course.

With this astrological awareness, every individual is given their own personalized **12-Step *AA program***. Each step defines the attitudes and actions that will be needed, to pursue one's creative endeavors.

In this process, each step repeatedly leads to the next, in a logical order. Each shift in Polarity and Mode brings a transformation into a different state or "condition" of being.

In sequential order, these 12 Zodiac Signs describe the physical, mental, emotional and spiritual steps that will be needed—to bring any creative endeavor into completion!

These 12 steps also can help individuals to find the wholeness that will bring health, happiness and the fulfillment of their purpose on Earth. The starting point of any creative adventure is symbolized in the Cardinal Mode and fiery Spirit of the Sign **Aries**.

(1) ARIES: *Go for it!* ,

In any awakening moment, the rising light allows every individual to see—*"where things are going and what actions need to be taken".*

With that clarity, the gates are open, as the Cardinal Fire of Aries lights the path ahead—to start a new adventure of self-discovery.

(2) TAURUS: *Use common sense.*

Whoa! Stop the charge and come to your senses! With the seeing eyes of Aries, Taurus' senses of touch, smell, taste and hearing are activated, to help us understand *what is real.*

With Fixed Earth skills, you can do the work and build the structure—that will make life more comfortable.

(3) GEMINI: *Understand the input from your senses !*

With the injection of the expansive force of Mutable Air, the mind is activated—to loosen the grip and analyze the input from your Taurus senses. With the learning of words and language, you can describe the differences between all things, and then communicate *what you know* to others.

(4) CANCER: *Turn ideas into thoughtful feelings!*

When thoughts seem too complex, it is time to examine their meaning, and determine how they will impact the feelings of the families and friends in your neighborhood.

If everything feels good, one can move out of their shelter of their home, and begin the interaction with their neighbors and environment. Your Leo friends will likely make the introductions.

⑤ LEO: *Create the visions, that you feel in your heart!*

Every individual needs to define the uniqueness of his/her **Aries** identity. This task begins when individuals present their "personal visions" to others. This desire is readily seen in Leos—who proudly step up onto any stage—to present their grandiose insights on how to make their neighborhoods more playful and colorful.

This Fixed Fire is in every individual, for we all need to receive recognition for the work that we contribute in our numerous fields of pursuit.

⑥ VIRGO: *Let's make things work!*

Leo's vision looks fabulous, but will it work? To find out, let's bring in the work ethic of **Taurus** and the mind of **Gemini**—to put the pieces into workable form. It is the **Mutable Earth** of **Virgo**, that inspires us to do the work, that will serve the needs of others.

⑦ LIBRA: *Partner with others to refine your creations!*

When the knowledge and experiences of others are considered, the input brings an array of refined and valuable works. When they are shared equally with all of the contributors, the creative power is multiplied.

⑧ SCORPIO: *Hold on to your deeply held convictions!*

In this joining, there's an emotional connection with others. It reveals what is truly valuable, and what needs to be held onto! It also shows what needs to be discarded. This creates the magical transformations, that will bring new forms of creation into being.

⑨ SAGITTARIUS: *Free yourself from all attachments!*

With the letting go of self-imposed limits, individuals are free to pursue visions, far greater than their own.

Here, we can recognize that we live in an abundant Universe, that can provides joy and bounty for all.

Yes, anything is possible!

⑩ CAPRICORN: *Build upon the wisdom, that was gathered.*

With the collective efforts of others, from past generations, many of our institutions were built—to support and comfort our **Cancer** families.

With the teaching of past lessons—and the passing on of newly gathered wisdom—the future looks bright!

With this belief in future goals, we can work to make it happen. It's all *thumbs up* from here!

⑪ AQUARIUS: *See the light at the end of the tunnel!*

With this optimistic view, things are looking brighter, every day. This suggests that an *All-Knowing Intelligence* is piloting this ship in space—and it is feeding us the inventive ideas—that will bring needed future changes!

With this gathering of friendly minds, our collective hopes and wishes can form the new ideas—that will make our dreams a reality!

⑫ PISCES: *Believe that YOU are part of a grander plan.*

With the increasing light, the melting snow and Aquarius' affirmations, it is time to recognize that it is the end of Winter—and another yearly cycle of life has ended! This stirs the emotions *and it piques the imagination of many souls*— to prepare for a new round of creation.

More than others, this Mutable Water Sign feels the multitude of currents, that are occurring here on Earth and in the heavens above. These sensitive souls recognize how every event affects all of the others, asnd how our past actions influence all of our future creations. With Pisces, past and future are the same, and everything is captured in the NOW. With this, it is time to begin another round of creation—and move into the future, with the Cardinal Fire of **Aries**.

CELEBRITY SNAPSHOTS

Selected Articles from

1996 to 2020, a monthly column by William Schreib

"Celebrity Snapshots" begin in the January 1996 issue of *Dell Horoscope, the World's Leading Astrology Magazine*. It continued as a monthly column until January of 2020, the magazine's last issue. In these 23 years, *Snapshots* of the astrological makeups of over 250 different celebrities were created by the author of this book.

In this book's finale, 24 of those *Dell Horoscope Snapshots* are presented. Each *Snapshot* contains a collage of photos, that shows the subject's Sun, Moon and Ascendant. Some also discuss the effects of their planetary placements and aspects.

Some photos were updated and the text was rewritten to show how the components in each *Snapshot* was reflected in the previous or following celebrity's chart. A collection of 235 celebrities can be viewed in Schreib's 2018 book *"Portaits of Personality".*

~~~

Special thanks goes to DELL HOROSCOPE'S Editor-in-Chief Ronnie Grishman, who give me the opportunity to pursue this creative adventure. It also could not have been done without the efforts of DELL's Senior Editor Edward Kajkowski, whose editorial skills and astrological knowledge taught me how to improve my writing over the years.

William Schreib

Snapshots: Aries Sun Signs

Lady Gaga
(Stefani Germanotta)
3/28/1986, 5:07 P.M. , 9:53 A.M.
Yonkers, N.Y.

Early on, Stephani Germanotta was insecure and terrified of performing in front of others—a likely consequence of her Sun's square (or distancing) from its ruling planet Mars. Fortunately, Stefani's Sun is at the top of her chart. This (and her many Neptune and lunar aspects) likely inspired her to redirect the once obstructed light of her Sun—to set the world on fire, with the illusions of her alter ego: "*Lady Gaga*".

This lady displays the physical traits of the Aries Ram—notably the arched eyebrows and eyes that sweep up on the sides. The long and convex face is also obvious.

Ascendant: Gemini

Stefani's original birth time gave her a Virgo Ascendant. A newer birth time gives her Gemini rising. Her "non-virgin" persona suggests that her Ascendant is the latter Mutable Sign. In the LR photo, we see her in a "non-performing state". There, her inactive flesh reveals the underlying bone structure of Gemini—i.e., the broad frontal teeth of a rabbit, the offset brows and eyes—and the rectangular jaw that juts out from the upper half of the face. These are features common with Gemini.

Gaga's Gemini Ascendant is opposed by Mars, Neptune and Uranus. The latter two trine Gaga's Venus in Aries. This supports her shocking public persona. All three oppose her Ascendant. This gives Gaga the drive and the inventive creative skills to build her outrageous and constantly-changing personas—that run the gamut from "beautiful glam" to "techno-metallic" and all the way to disturbingly bizarre. Who can forget her gross dress, entirely covered with raw meat? These grotesque images were likely inspired by her Moon.

Moon in Scorpio:
Gaga's Pluto conjoins her Moon in Scorpio. These two components also sextile Neptune. This gives Gaga a powerful sense of fantasy, as well as the emotional strength to conquer the world with her daring imagery. The LL photo shows the power, intensity and grossness of Pluto's conjunction with her Scorpio Moon. These two components are activated in Gaga's theatrical 5th House of creativity. With their trine to Jupiter on her MC, her public finds her work disturbing—but also outrageously hilarious!

Rachel Maddow
4 / 1 / 19734, 12:23 P.M.
Hayward, CA

SUN: Aries
With rapid fire delivery, the Cardinal Fire of Rachel's Sun delivers MSNBC's news reports to her fans.

With her Sun, Venus, Moon and Mercury residing in her philosophical 9th House —and her Sun's trine to Neptune in Sagittarius (sextiling her Mars and Jupiter in altruistic Aquarius), Maddow has a gift for developing very complex ideas and delivering a grander overview. With this, many of her fans see her as a calm voice in the storm; Her rivals see her as being aggressive and highly opinionated.

Moon in Pisces:
Maddow's Moon and Mercury are in Pisces. This gives her an ability to walk in the shoes of others and sense the nature of their feelings. Notably, these two components square Saturn, while the ringed planet trines Uranus in Libra. This installs a sense of fairness and a enduring faith in humanity. Saturn also sextiles her Sun. This gives her the sense of authority and substance that she needs, since she has no Earth in her chart.

In emotional moments, Rachel's lunar forces take control. Note how the fiery eyes are doused by the water, as her hard-edged Ram features are hidden by the rounded, saturated flesh. The patterns of mutability are also apparent as they skew and twist the vertical lines of Maddow's Ram-like face. The resulting expressions resemble the features, that we saw in the Sign of Pisces.

In her show, these undulating emotions of Pisces became obvious, when Rachel does her weekend "cocktail party". Watch how she escapes into her fantasy land, mixing a drink while imagining she's sharing it with a friend.

Cancer Ascendant:
When Rachel's lunar lights recede, the Cardinal Force returns once again, but instead of the headstrong outward charge of Aries, the forces are drawing her downward—into the watery base of the ocean below. This reverse in polarity is seen in the rare moments when this Ram becomes emotional and "lost for words". Physically, this Rising Sign gives Rachel the round Full Moon temples of the Cancer crab.

Snapshots: Taurus Sun Signs

Jack Nicholson
April 22, 1937, 11:00 A.M.
Neptune N.J.

Taurus Sun: The features of Jack Nicholson's Taurus Sun can be seen in his bovine eyes, wide nostrils and in the cowlicks on the sides of the head. (They mock the ears of a steer). The looks are there, but few would guess he has five components in Earth Signs. For this is not a contented beast, calmly grazing in a field. He smells the smoke in the air and red flags of Fire are waving in his face. This fire is ignited by the ruler of Jack's Sun—**Venus**! It's in the **Fire Sign** of **Aries**, conjoining his **Sun** and **Uranus** *in his 10th House.* With this, Jack became "a star" by presenting his assertive and erratic image to the public.

Leo Ascendant: When Leo rises, Jack's eyes turn from bovine to feline, and his jaw juts down to reveal the Lion's once hidden jowls. In this moment, Jack holds the fire—to purr and preen and assure himself that everything is in control. This control is enhanced by his **Ascendant**'s conjunction to **Pluto** and their T-square to Jupiter and the Sun/Venus/Uranus cluster on his Midheaven. His Ascendant also trines his **Sagittarius Mars**. This gives him the fiery and scattered metabolism (that in its clumsiness) warns us of the dangers of putting a bull in a china shop.

The placement of Pluto near his Ascendant (and its six other aspects) empowers all of his other components. With Pluto is in the Sign of **Cancer**, this leaves an odd feeling, that some disturbing force is percolating just below Jack's theatrical facade. In *"The Last Detail"*, his Leo mask was front and center— roaring for attention! In his Oscar winning role in *"One Flew Over The Cuckoo's Nest"*, he showed us a loud and proud individual, who made us wonder who was really insane. In *"The Shining"*, Pluto took over and there was no doubt.

Moon in Virgo: When emotionally riled, Virgo Moons often become nervous and obsessed with frivolous details, but when they interact with others, they are often very proper in their manners. Not so with Jack, for his **Moon's sextile to Pluto** prompts all courtesy to fly out the window! Recall the restaurant scene in *"Five Easy Pieces"* when Jack reorders his breakfast. Watch his questioning responses in *"Chinatown"* or his hypochondriac character in *"As Good As It Gets"* who's consumed by life's imperfections. What you see are the reactions of a Virgo Moon.

Renee Zellweger
4/25/1969, 2:41 PM, Katy, Texas

Taurus Sun: In *"Cinderella Man"* and *"Cold Mountain"*, Zellweger played roles that showed her earthy nature. In the first film, her role as a downtrodden depression-era wife demanded little flash and intensity. In her Oscar winning *"Cold Mountain"* role, she showed the bullheaded stubbornness of a back wood's girl, determined to "make something of herself". In these films, she showed the physical traits of her Taurus Sun. Note the fixed eyebrows, the stubby, wide-based nose, the firmly set brows and eyes, the square forehead and jaw and Taurus' sensuous lips.

Leo Moon: After seeing Zellweger's showy performance in the dazzling film *"Chicago"*, one can suspect that she has Leo in her chart. It's her Moon!

This fiery nature was seen in Nicholson's theatrical persona. In contrast, Renee's lion qualities are see in her lunar reactions. When she reacts to the solar expressions of others, their fiery responds often become fixed, dramatic and theatrical. Notably, her **Venus** in **Aries** and her **Mars** is in **Sagittarius**—the same as Nicholson. The difference is that Renee's two personal planets form a grand trine with her **Moon** and **Mars,** not to her Ascendant. Her emotional reactions are far more dramatic, than what we see in Nicolson's fussy Virgo Moon.

Virgo Rising/Strong Mercury: Renne's Jupiter conjoins Pluto and Uranus in the Sign of Virgo. All three (save for Uranus) are in her **1st House**— trining her **9th House Mercury**.

In her interviews, Renee's eyes blink rapidly, as her hands and fingers become animated. These are products of the strong Mercury aspects in her chart. These mercuric gifts (and her Mercury's placement in the philosophical 9th House) enables her to connect to the voices of distant cultures. As we saw in Renee's roles as *"Bridget Jones"* and *"Miss Potter"*, this enabled her to master the language, tones and accents from two different periods of history.

Snapshots: Gemini Sun Signs

Mercury's wings fluttered in anticipation, when CNN began its 24 hour daily news cycle. When they added their split-screen images, rapid video edits and the constant scroll of "news" at the bottom of the screen, the *Winged Messenger* became ecstatic! Finally, every Mortal Being could get their daily "Mercury jolt"—just by tuning into this channel of streaming information.

To top it off, CNN made Anderson Cooper an anchor! With the electric and smooth-flowing tongue of his **Gemini Sun**—the words flowed out into the land, for all to hear. The Greek God Hermes was also very pleased.

In full solar expression, Anderson eyelids flap rapidly—creating the illusion that there are "two blinks instead of one". Watch how his mouth, nose and chin twist in alternate directions—when he delivers his unemotional, fast-paced questions to his guests. This quickness of mind is enhanced by his **Sun's trine** to his **Ascendant/Mars conjunction** in **Libra**, and their opposition to his martial **Aries Moon.**

Moon in Aries: Watch what happens, when Anderson tries to prod his guests for more answers. Note how his head abruptly butts forward, and how his eyebrows lift up on the outer edges—when he reacts to and counters his subject's comments. His emotional response is often short and to the point, perhaps a simple "What do you mean?". If the tension becomes overwhelming, Cooper's wide Libra smile often rises to the surface, to calm the conversation.

Anderson Cooper
6/3/1967, 3:46 P.M.
New York, NY

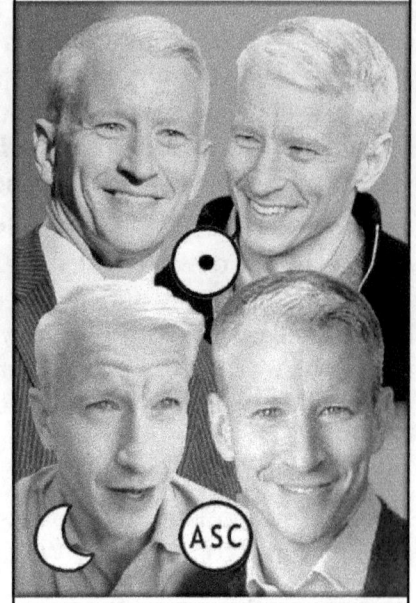

Libra Ascendant: In moments of non-expression or interaction, the swirling winds of Cooper's Sun and fiery Moon are quelled by the calm breezes of his Cardinal Air Ascendant. The lower left photo shows the wide squinted eyes, the dimpled V-lined chin and the charming smile of Cooper's Libra mask. However, that pleasantry does not last for long, for Mars conjoins his Rising Sign and both components trine Venus, the ruler of Libra.

Nicole Kidman
6/20/1967, 3:15 P.M. Honolulu, HA

Gemini Sun: Nicole's Gemini Sun is in the **8th House** and its only aspect is its trine to her **Scorpio Ascendant.** This is why her mercuric expressions are so hidden and controlled. With her Sun's ruler **Mercury**, **sextile** a **Pluto/Uranus conjunction** in the Mercury-ruled **Sign of Virgo**, her mercuric circuits often change frequency and voltage. This gives her a trembling low-pitched voice. The erratic electricity be seen in her darting eyes and in her animated hands and fingers.

Sagittarius Moon: Kidman's Moon has **6 major aspects.** (Seven, if you count her *Leo Midheaven*). Her Centaur Moon squares the previously mentioned Pluto/Uranus conjunction—while it forms a grand trine to her Venus, Saturn and her Moon's ruling planet **Jupiter**. This Moon also sextiles Mars in Libra.

These aspects kick up the fires, as they make her reactions daringly blunt and free of inhibitions. They also give her a gift for performing a diverse range of roles—that run the gamut from action fantasies, musicals, comedies and dramas. *Batman Forever, Moulin Rouge, Bewitched* and *Cold Mountain* are good examples. Also, Pluto's aspects to her two luminaries instills an aura of mystery. This seductive nature is reinforced by her Fixed Water Ascendant.

Scorpio Ascendant: Notably, Kidman's **29° Gemini Sun trines** her **Scorpio Ascendant.** Gemini's ruler **Mercury** also trines her **1st House Neptune**, while it also **sextiles her Uranus/Pluto conjunction** in **Virgo**. These connections to her Ascendant explain Nicole's unusual and *other-worldly appearance!*

The Jupiter Effect: With her high-placed hips, Nicole's upper torso appears smaller than normal, while the lower half appears extra long. She appears to be—*all arms and legs!*

Since the Sign of Sagittarius is ruled by Jupiter—and this planet exaggerates everything it touches—we need to find the aspects and placement of Jupiter in Nicole's chart. With her **Jupiter** in Sagittarius' *9th House home*, trining her *Sagittarius Moon*, the lower half of her body is greatly enlarged, since the lower hips and thighs are ruled by the Sign of Sagittarius. Her abnormally long arms may be due Mercury's (her Sun's ruler) sextile to Uranus.

Snapshots: Cancer Sun Signs

Meryl Streep
6/22/1949 / 8:05 A.M., Summit, NJ

Meryl's face displays many of the Crab's physical traits. Her most noticeable features are her round lunar temples and the bulging triangle between the brows. What is different is her demeanor. Meryl has her Sun conjoining Uranus and sextiling Saturn. This gives Streep her delightfully irregular expressions. Fortunately, they are never too bizarre—for her Saturn aspect always keeps them in control.

In *Sophie's Choice* and *Out of Africa*, we saw Meryl's gift for articulating the rhythms, dialects and structural tones in various language and cultures. This gift can be attributed to her **Mercury/Mars conjunction** in **Gemini** and their trine to **Neptune**. These three planet's sextile to Pluto empowers her verbal skills, while Pluto's square to her Moon gives her a gift for controlling her emotional content.

Fixed Taurus Moon:
Meryl's Taurus Moon keeps her emotions well anchored and her interactions with others are often firmly Fixed. Note how her nostrils widen, as the eyes drop down on the outer edges—to create the look of a contented bovine. These sensual emotions are further stabilized by her Moon's exact square to Pluto and its sextile to Taurus' ruler: Venus. Meryl's emotions are incredibly powerful and totally controlled. All of this is dramatically presented through the screen of her Leo Ascendant.

Fixed Leo Ascendant:
In the film *Prada*, Meryl's Fixed and Fiery mask was fully displayed on center stage, as she displayed her aura of confidence—and dispersed her royal decrees! Notably, with Neptune (the ruler of cinema) sextiling her 1st House Pluto, Meryl became her era's most powerful Hollywood Star. As of 2021, she has won 2 Oscars, for Best Actress.

Benedict Cumberbatch 7/19/1976, 12:00 P.M., London, UK

With six masculine components, Benedict shows little of the emotions of water. Still, in the right moments, his Cancer Sun's waters will surge upward, to crest and round his facial flesh. At this peak, the tide reverses direction to return to the ocean's floor below. (This rise and fall is displayed in the two upper photos).

Benedict waters appears to be far more driven, than what we see in *Meryl Streep*—for his 3 key components are **all in Cardinal Signs**. Also, his **Cancer Sun conjoins Mercury, Venus** and **Saturn**, but those planets are in **fiery Leo**, not Cancer. These four components also T-square his Moon and Uranus. This array of dynamic aspects affects the nature of his lunar and solar expressions.

Aries Moon:
Amazingly, this crab's **Aries Moon** is part of a giant **Grand T-square**—that also includes his Sun, Mercury, Venus Saturn and **Uranus**. With this powerful arrangement, his reactions are often assertive and militant—yet, also distant and emotionally detached! The aggressive qualities were seen in his roles as an officer in *War Horse* and the secret agent in *Tinter Taylor Soldier Spy*. The emotional distance was on full display in his roll as *Sherlock Holmes*.

The LR photo shows how these martial forces push the forehead forcefully to the front; This raise the eyes and brows up on the outer edges. Since Mars is the ruler of Aries and Cumberbatch's Mars is in the Earthy Sign of Virgo, we see why his physical actions often appear fastidious, rather than aggressive in nature.

Libra Ascendant:
With this Cardinal Air **Ascendant**, Benedict's Sun, Mercury, Venus and Saturn are all in his **10th House** of career. Thusly, Benedict became known for his powerful mercuric persona and his many highly cerebral roles—that we saw in BBC's *Sherlock Holmes* and in the TV movie *Hawking*, where he played the genius mathematician *Alan Turing*, the designer of the first computer.

With Pluto on his Ascendant and *Saturn being his most aspected planet*, we see why Benedict spend a year-long sabbatical in India, teaching English in a monastery. **These heavy Saturn** and **Pluto links** also gave him the intense and stoney persona, that we saw in his role in as *Dr. Strange*.

When Benedict's Sun and Moon are in repose, Libra's wide V-shaped smile and the sparkling, squinted eyes of Libra rise up into full display. In these moments, he appears markedly pleasant and surprisingly relaxed.

Snapshots: Leo Sun Signs

Barack Obama
8/4/1961, 7:24 P.M.
Honolulu, HI

Leo Sun:
Of the 44 US Presidents, Barack was one of the 18 who had a Fixed Sun Sign. The top Fixed Signs to be elected were Scorpio and Aquarius. They each share 5 wins; Taurus and Leo have 4 each. This tells us this country likes a "fixed and stable anchor" to run the country. Unlike some of the others, Obama's Fixed Leo Sun give him a extra flair of showmanship.

Barrack's first gained national attention, as an off-night speaker at the 2004 Democratic convention. There, he showed the proud stance of a Lion, as he presented his vision on how to build a better America. Four years later, he became the Democratic candidate and then President of the United States.

As President, Obama held frequent press conferences and gave many major national speeches. His eloquence for presenting complex social issues made him a popular President. These communicative skills are a product of his Mercury, Venus and Gemini Moon.

Gemini Moon:
With his **Mercury** in **Leo** (conjoined his Sun), Obama found the right words, to verbalize the visions in his mind. **Mercury's sextile** to his **Moon** and its trine to his **Jupiter/Saturn conjunction** (in Aquarius and Capricorn), gave his words scope and substance. His Venus in Cancer and its trine to Neptune give his voice emotional clarity. This conjunction's trine to his Mars (in Virgo) was the methadone, that regulated the abnormally precise cadence of his voice.

Aquarius Ascendant:
"Hope"" was the word that symbolized Obama's first campaign and his ideals for a brighter future. This optimism can be attributed to Obama's **12th House Jupiter** in **Aquarius** and the fact that Jupiter and Saturn are the only planets on the left side of his chart. His life was one of destiny!

With Aquarius as his view to the world, Obama was able to see both ends of the political spectrum. It helped him find the right people to reverse a major economic crash, and pass major Health Care and Civil Rights legislation. His actions were revolutionary, but they also sparked a counter-revolution! That is what we expect from Aquarius.

J. K. Rowling
July 31, 1965 / 9:10 P.M. Bristol, UK

Leo Sun:
The light of Rowling's Leo Sun gave her an ability to envision her tales of bravery and friendship—all in a manner that would excite the creative spirit and empowerment of children. The success as a writer was supported by her **Leo Sun's trine** to her playful and spiritual **Sagittarius Midheaven**—and its square to Venus, Uranus and Pluto in mercuric Virgo.

Four Components and a Moon in Virgo:
Rowling's Moon and Mercury are also in the Sign of Virgo, and this gives her 5 Virgo components. They all are clustered in her **7th House**! With all this, and a Mutable Jupiter and Saturn, we see why J.K. lacks many of the Fixed physical traits of the lion.

J.K.'s **Virgo planets** makes her verbal skills precise and very detailed. Virgo's critical nature was seen in the imperfections of her characters, and in her definition of the social ethics, student rivalries and institutional incompetencies. No one was perfect.

Rowling's **Saturn** and **Jupiter** both have **7 major aspects**. **Saturn**'s placement in **Pisces** coats her critical solar observations in a blanket of compassion, while Jupiter in **Gemini** decrees that she has a giant gift for finding the right words to create her seven *Harry Potter* books. This Leo's words stirred the imaginations of people of all ages.

Aquarius Ascendant:
The Fixed Air of Rowling's **Aquarius Ascendant** is empowered by its grand trine to her **Libra Mars** and **Gemini Jupiter**. When J.K.'s fiery Leo light dims, her Aquarian eyes light up and leave the room—to focus on a distant place in space. There, she intuitively locks into the universe of words—inside and outside her head.' In these moments, J.K.'s facial flesh relaxes, to reveal the underlying cubical bone structure of her Ascendant. In this moment, all of the Mutable features in her face disappear!

NOTE: *Like Obama, J.K. has only one planet on the left side of her chart. Both were driven by forces, greater than their own.*

Snapshots: Virgo Sun

Amy has the same Signs as J.K. Rowling, but they're in different components.

Amy Poehler
9/16/1971, 4:33 P.M.
Newton, MA

Virgo Sun: With her Sun, Mercury, Venus and Pluto in Virgo, the energy of Mutable Earth dominates Amy's mannerisms and solar expressions. The Upper Right photo shows how the mercuric forces of her Mutable Sun skews the flesh— to create her offset and angled facial features.

However, Amy's four Virgo components are the only passively-charged Signs in her chart—and often, her Sun is over powered by the **5 Air components** in her chart. This includes her Aquarius Ascendant.

Aquarius Ascendant: Amy's Fixed Air Ascendant forms a grand trine with Saturn and Pluto. Also, her 1st House Aquarius Mars forms a second grand trine with Saturn and Neptune—all in Air Signs! This abundance of Air was seen in Amy's flighty and quixotic characters on *Saturday Night Live*. Also, with Jupiter conjunct Neptune in Sagittarius (near her Midheaven), it was appropriate that she achieved great recognition in the field of comedy.

Leo Moon: When Amy becomes emotional, her flesh reshapes—to form the cubical features of her Leo Moon. Note how Amy's head rises, and how her hands suddenly cling close to her proud, expanding chest—rather than hover nervously around her Virgo-ruled midsection. In this moment, her jaw is firmly set to the front. This pulls the cheeks and chin upward and it shortens the long Virgo face. As the LR photos shows, this creates the confident pose of a lion.

Jimmy Fallon 9/19/1974
6:21 P.M. Bay Ridge, NY

Poehlar's has 7 components in Masculine Signs. In contrast, Jimmy Fallon has 6 planets in Passive Signs, including his three key lights. With all of these, Jimmy's nature is far more gentle, than what we saw in Amy.

Sun in Virgo: Fallon's only Earth is his Virgo Sun and Venus; These earthy qualities are diffused, since they are part of the six planets in his Venus and Libra-ruled 7th House. This infusion of Air accounts for Fallon's Venusian "Libra smile". Note how the horizontal spread of Libra remove the skewed facial lines of his Mutable Sun. That's why the worried and mercuric nature of his Virgo Sun is rarely seen.

Moon in Scorpio: Jimmy's Moon is in the Pisces decan of Scorpio—and it forms a Grand Water Trine with Saturn in Cancer and his Ascendant/Jupiter conjunction in **Pisces**. Jupiter's placement in this triad of water allows him to present a free flowing mix of emotions—with little sense of Scorpio's intensity. This also gives him a remarkable gift for voicing and impersonating the rhythmic cadences and personalities of others.

Fallon's Venus (in Virgo) sextiles his Moon and Saturn in Water Signs. This triad (and the cluster of Libra planets) makes Jimmy's Scorpio Moon easy-going. He rarely gets emotional on his evening "love-fest" show.

Pisces Ascendant: Venus (the planet of love) opposes Fallon's Jupiter and Ascendant. These components are T-shared by Neptune (the ruler of his calculated Pisces Ascendant). Jupiter's placement on this "front gate" accounts for Jimmy's gift for humor and his caffeine driven persona. With his Mutable Water mask, Jimmy is the "least agressive" of the late night talk show hosts. He was ridiculed for not engaging in the political ranting, that came after the 2016 USA election.

With his Ascendant in the Mutable Water Sign of Pisces, Jimmy's body structure is somewhat plump—and not what we'd expect from a normally lanky Virgo Sun, or with someone with Jupiter on the Ascendant. Fallon's lack of Mutable features can be attributed to his cluster of Libra planets and his Cancer Saturn--all are in Cardinal Signs! Also, his Pisces Jupiter and Ascendant are in the Cardinal decan of Cancer.

[*On February 18, 2015, Jimmy Fallon replaced Jay Leno as the host of NBC's The Tonight Show. Using this moment and nine other events, astrologer Isaac Starkman created a rectified chart to determine Jimmy's Pisces Ascendant].

Snapshots: Libra Sun Signs

Bruno Mars
(Peter Gene Hernandez)
10/8/1985, 3:56 P.M. Waikiki, HI

Bruno Mars' career began as a member of a record and music writing team. They were named the "Biggest Songwriters of 2010" by *Music Week* magazine. In that same year, Bruno's first album *Doo-Wops and Hooligans* was completed with the help of his creative team. In this work, he showed his dynamic flare of Fire, his delightful mix of lyrics (Air) and the inspiring rhythms of Water. Many of these tunes were performed at the 2015 Super Bowl.

Libra Sun: Bruno's airy Libra Sun accounts for his need to create ideas and to collaborate with others. These easy-going energies also explain why his music shows little of the aggression expected in hip-hop. Some call his work "friendly-pop".

On this album, we heard Bruno's high-pitched, airy and breathy voice, as well as the soothing, loving and melodic tones of Libra. Visually, Bruno displays many of the regular physical features of Libra, notably the wide-set eyes and V-lined smile.

Leo Moon: Youngsters with Leo Moons are often desirous of attracting the attention of others. These lion impulses drove Bruno to perform at a very young age. Since children tend to initially express the needs of their Moon, readers should check Bruno's video on the internet, where he struts on state at the age of four. It is this Leo Moon that adds a flare of elegance to his performances. It may also account for his many hats, that proudly serve as his royal crown.

Pisces Ascendant: The other worldly appearance, that we saw in Jimmy Fallon, is also seen in Bruno, since both have Pisces Ascendants. Bruno's skewed bone structure is more obvious, since his Ascendant forms a snug trine to Neptune, while Fallon's forms a square. This relaxation of the facial flesh reveals the underlying bone structure, that tilts Bruno's dreamy eyes onto the sides of the face. This gives him a portal view of two different worlds.

This receptive mask (and his Libra Sun) enables Bruno to create the music, that inspires people to dance together and be in harmony with different cultures from around the world. It is, as NPR music critic Ann Powers stated: "A part of the art that offers humanity....a glimpse of a better world, or at least a happier one."

Kate Winslet
10/5/1975, 7:15 A.M.
Reading, UK

For years, this author wanted to make Winslet one of my Snapshot subjects—but she didn't seem to "show any of the physical traits of a triple Libra". This was before this author discovered the influence of the decans. [The decans of all Signs were explored on page 70].

Sun, Moon and Ascendant in Libra

The first **1°** to **9°** of Libra present the true essence of Libra—but Winslet's Sun, Ascendant and Moon are respectively 10, 11 and 13 degrees—all are in the **2nd decan of Libra**. This decan instills some of the qualities of the next Sign in the Air Element's trilogy—in this case, the **Fixed Air of Aquarius!** This explains why Kate has many of the features of Aquarius, rather than Libra.

As demonstrated in her photos, Kate shows little of the billowing facial lines that we see in the Libra caricature. Also, her features do not "spread freely to the sides"—they seem to mock the funneling Fixity of Aquarius. The V-lined smile and well-proportioned features of Libra are missing-- and her facial features appear to be concentrated in the center. This creates the dimples in the center of the cheeks. In between, the square-tipped nose and wide-set nostrils sit over the tight *down-drawn lower lip*. That is Aquarius' most obvious physical feature!

The top photo shows hints of the horizontally-spread eyes of Kate's Libra Sun. The lower images show the influence of her other Aquarius decans. The one on the lower left appears to be one of her lunar reactions. The neutral expression in the LR photo, reveals the cubical bone structure of her Libra/Aquarius decan Ascendant.

Other Planetary Considerations: *Pluto conjoins* Kate's **Sun, Moon** and **Ascendant**. With this, and her three Fixed Air decan components, this triple Libra was able to play her emotionally powerful roles in "*Revolutionary Road*" and "*The Reader*". With her Venus' sextile to Uranus—despite her huge fame in "*Titanic*"—Kate was drawn to star in low-pay "off-beat art house films", such as "*Eternal Sunshine of the Spotless Mind*".

Snapshots: Scorpio Sun Signs

Leonardo DiCaprio
11/11/1974, 2:47 A.M.
Hollywood, CA

Libra Moon and Ascendant: Like Kate Winslet, DiCaprio has a Libra Moon and Ascendant. However, he shows few of the pleasant qualities of Libra, that we saw, when he began his career playing the cheery kid in TV's *Growing Pains*. Later, Libra's charm was seen in his film *Romeo and Juliet*—however, most of his roles are intense and powerful. *This shows us the difference between a Libra and Scorpio Sun.*

Scorpio Sun: Leonardo's **Sun, Mercury, Venus and Uranus conjoin Mars** in his **2nd House.** All are in the Sign of **Scorpio**! With these connections and his Mars' Grand Trine with his Jupiter and Midheaven, Leo found many action driven roles. His films *Django Unchained, Gangs of New York* showed the violence. *The Revenant* demonstrated Scorpio's survival instincts. In *The Man In The Iron Mask*, the two sides of his Scorpio Sun and Libra Moon were seen in his duel roles, as an evil king and his fair-minded twin brother.

All of Leonardo's Libra and Scorpio components are clustered in his first two Houses. Saturn and Neptune are also on the left side of his chart. This leaves only *Jupiter on the right side of his chart*. This heavy left hemisphere makes DiCaprio highly self-driven. With the 5 Uranus conjunctions, he made many daring leaps in his career.

Leonardo's first breakthrough came with his Oscar-nominated role as a troubled teen in *What's Eating Gilbert Grape*. Shortly after, he went into the darker edges, playing a psychotic teen in *Marvin's Room*, a heroin addict in *The Basketball Diaries* and his controversial role as the gay poet Rimbaud in *Total Eclipse*.

Saturn is placed on DiCaprio's Midheaven. This suggests a delay in his receiving of earned recognition. In 2015, after six previous nominations, he finally won a "*Best Actor Oscar*" for his performance in *The Revenant*. This long-delayed reward came, when transiting Saturn was opposing his 10th House natal Saturn.

Goldie Hawn
11/21/1945, 9:20 A.M.
Washington Highlands, DC

"*Astrology is nonsense!*" That was what this author thought, back in 1974, when I read that Goldie was a Scorpio. This was not what the books described—for all I saw was a giggling chatterbox on NBC's "Laugh-In". Then, somewhere I found a copy of Goldie's chart and it showed me that she had a Gemini Moon and Sagittarius Ascendant. It showed me how these two key Mutable components could override her Scorpio Sun. This inspired me to gather more images, to find more physical clues. That is how this book began.

Sagittarius Rising: On NBC'S *Rowan and Martin's Laugh-In*, (1968-73), Goldie was the giggling hyena, whose animated mannerisms were certainly not Scorpio. However, this "Laugh-In" fan saw Hawn's lanky physical body, her large domed head, the long neck and the big horse-like eyes that swept up and to the sides of her face. These "horsey clues" helped this budding astrologer to understand that "we all are more than our Sun Signs".

Moon in Gemini: This *Mutable Air Moon* explains Goldie's high-pitched and breathy voice, her rapidly blinking eyes and her flying fingers—that seem to be animating the thoughts in her head. These gestures were elevated, when she *talked about her feelings*. It showed how one's emotions reflect the Sign of one's Moons.

I also noticed that Jupiter was at the top of Goldie's chart, trining her Moon and Uranus conjunction, while her Leo Mars trines her Sun. These aspects explained her theatrical physical metabolism, and the delightful quirks in her personality.

Scorpio Sun: At a young age, Goldie's **28° Scorpio Sun** *progressed into Sagittarius*. This Mutable Fires sparkled for 30 years—and they was on full display in her antics on *Laugh-In* and in her first film *Cactus Flower*. This film won her an Oscar for *Best Supporting Actress*. Our first true glimpse of this lady's Fixed Water was in her 1975 film *Shampoo*, where she played a rejected lover, who was determined to find her own personal power. Around 1978, **Hawn's Centaur Sun** progressed into **Capricorn**. In 1980, she became one of the first women to star in, produce and direct a film for a major studio. This film *Private Benjamin* was a huge hit! This was followed as produced nine other films and TV movies in the next decade. These tenacious qualities were also seen in her character in the 1996 film *First Wife's Club*.

Snapshots: Sagittarius Suns

Taylor Swift
12/13/1989, 8:36 P.M.
Wyomissing, PA

Sagittarius Sun: A 2017 *NY Times* review of Taylor Swift's music stated that she appears to be "more in touch with her inner life than most adults". Such philosophical pursuits are expected in most Centaurs, but rarely in someone in her 20's.

Swift's **21°** Centaur Sun is her only Fire Sign and its only aspect is its opposition to her Full Moon at **1°** Cancer. So why does she have this incredible drive to "understand herself"? It is likely due to her Moon and Jupiter's conjunction in the 8th House—and the fact that ALL of other components are on the LEFT SIDE of her chart. In this loaded hemisphere, the Sun (i.e., light of one's self) is building. Such people are driven to bring their personal light to full brightness.

That *NY Times* article also described Swift as "one of pop's finest songwriters and our country's foremost pragmatist." On her work on the album *Speak Now*, she stated "nothing is finished, until its written about"—while adding: "I think about my next move 10 steps ahead". This highly organized attitude can be attributed to her **Mercury, Neptune** and **Uranus**—all are **conjoined in** tenacious **Capricorn**. This empowers her Capricorn Saturn, that also conjoins her Mercury and Neptune. Her music comes from **Neptune's 7 aspects**—including its trine to her Midheaven.

Full Moon in Cancer: Taylor Swift was born on a Full Moon; It opposes her **21° Centaur Sun** and three of her Capricorn planets. Her Moon and Jupiter are the only components on the right side of her chart. With nine components on the Self-Directed Side of her chart, her creative efforts are all hers. Few contributions are needed from others.

Scorpio Ascendant: Taylor's Mars and Pluto conjoin her Scorpio Ascendant. Pluto (Scorpio's ruler) also sextiles her Saturn/Neptune conjunction in Capricorn. This empowered Neptune and Saturn instills the discipline, that make Taylor a prolific composer. Notably, Taylor's Ascendant is in the Cancer decan and with that Cancer Moon, she shows the wide delta between the eyebrows and the round lunar temples, that we see in most crabs.

Brad Pitt
12/18/1963, 6:31 A.M.
Shawnee, OK

Sun and Ascendant: Sagittarius The wild spirit of the Centaur ran freely in Brad's first major film role as the rebellious son in *A River Runs Through It*. This was the beginning of a career that grew in Jupiterian proportions—and it made him one of the super stars of his time! We saw the Archer's attraction to sports in Brad's ingenious baseball film: *Money Ball*. The Centaur's philosophical questions of life were examined in *Seven Years in Tibet* and *The Tree of Life*.

The upper photos show how the head rears up, when this Centaur kicks into action. Oddly, this unconstrained exuberance and joy was rarely seen in Brad's film performances. In the films *Ocean's 11, 12 and 13,* Brad was the markedly cool and restrained "straight man", who fed his practical observations to others. This nature is likely due to the six Earth Components in Brad's chart. They include his Moon.

Moon in Capricorn: Pitt's Moon conjoins Mercury and Venus in Capricorn. His Moon and Mercury also sextile Neptune in Scorpio, while his Capricorn Mars trines his Pluto/Uranus conjunction in his 9th House. That is why Brad is so mentally attracted to films with strong Pluto and Neptunian overtones. He was the tale teller in *Interview with the Vampire*, the obsessed detective in *Seven,* the institutionalized patient in *Twelve Monkeys* and the leader of *Inglorious Basterds*.

The presence of six components in Earth Signs explains Brad's grounded and staid disposition. It is his Moon and Mars in Capricorn, that gives him the emotional reactions and physical movements of a goat.

The LL photo shows what happens when Brad becomes reacts to others. Note how the flesh on the upper cheek bones builds into the stoney mounds, that push his eyes upward—to place them tightly under the ledge of his rigid brows. This gives him a very serious appearance.

With his Cardinal Earth Mars and his red planet's square to Jupiter (his Sun's ruling planet), Brad was given the extra physical stamina—to climb to the top of any mountain! With his Capricorn components and Saturn's square to Neptune, we see why Brad was attracted to his age-reversing lead role in the magical film: *The Curious Case of Benjamin Button*.

Snapshots: Capricorn Suns

Betty White
1/17/1922, 7:10 P.M.
Oak Park, IL

Capricorn Sun: It is said that many Capricorns reach their peaks late in life. Betty White's career supports this adage! This author recalls her being a panelist on TV's early game shows and a star in the '70's sitcom *The Mary Tyler Moore Show*. In the latter, her cranky character won her fame—and her first Emmy! In 2010 (in her 7th decade as a performer), Betty won another Emmy, serving as a host on *Saturday Night Live*. The latter came from an massive internet campaign from the youth of America, who convinced producers to make Betty a guest MC on the show. *That is how we show respect for our elders!*

In 2018, Betty completed the voicing of her character in the 2019 movie *Toy Story 4*. On December 21, 2021, just two weeks before her 100th birthday, she passed away. This endurance supports the adage that "work keeps Capricorns going".

Virgo Moon: Betty was also known for her role as "Rose" in *The Golden Girls*. In this gig, she played a delightfully ditsy and obsessively fussy character. This role truly reflected the mercuric lunacy of her Virgo Moon. The lower right photo shows how Betty's face rearranges—when her stony solar gaze transforms, to present the quizzical expression and skewed facial lines of her Virgo Moon.

Leo Ascendant: Betty began her career at 17, as her Leo Ascendant opened the doors to what would be a long and distinguished theatrical career. Betty's Rising Sign was seen, when she strutted into the room. It showed her aura of confidence and boastful persona. It often gave the impression that royalty had just arrived! This showy mask adds warmth (and a fiery spirt) to Betty's chilly solar light. Physically, it infuses her cubical forehead, thick mane and feline jowls—all attributes of a lion!

Muhammad Ali
1/17/1942. 6:30 P.M.
Louisville, KY

"Champions aren't made in gyms. Champions are made from something they have deep inside them: a desire, a dream, a vision. They have to have the last-minute stamina, the skill and the will, but the will must be stronger than the skill."—**Muhammad Ali**

Capricorn Sun: Capricorn goats know what it takes to reach the top, but their real status comes from what they do with their success. Ali became the World Heavyweight Boxing Champion at the age of twenty-two, but many say that his greatest achievements came later in life. Though hampered by his Parkinson's disease, Ali traveled around the world, to contribute to causes and fight against poverty, social inequities and racism.

At his career peak, Ali displayed the physical strength of a bull. This likely comes from his Midheaven Taurus Mars and its T-square to his Sun and Pluto. It was his Fixed Mars and Moon that gave him the focus to develop and master his boxing skill. Meanwhile, it was the Fixed Fire of his Leo Ascendant that gave him the *will and the desire*, to manifest the success, that he envisioned.

Leo Ascendant: *"I am the greatest!"*

Ali shouted this repeatedly, when he won the world's championship. In this moment of elation, the Fixed Fire of Leo rose to the surface—as it overrode his cautious Sun. There, as the fires intensified, Ali became even louder with each proclamation! This demonstrates how a Leo Rising Sign can ignite and inflate a person's sense of pride, when they present their mask to the others.

Aquarius Moon: *"I float like a butterfly. Sting like a bee."*

This famous reactive taunt to one of Ali's opponents, shows us the quirky reactions that we'd expect from an Aquarius Moon. It was this Moon (as well as the input of his Aquarius Mercury and Venus) that led him to change his name from Cassius Clay to Muhammad Ali, announce his new religion and then declare himself to be a conscientious objector to the military draft. In 1967, the riled establishment took away his title.

In 1970, the ban was lifted and in 1974, he regained his title. After ending his boxing career, Ali's humanitarian Moon lead him to build the **Muhammad Ali Center** In in Louisville, KY. This facility exhibits Ali's six core principles of confidence, conviction, dedication, giving, respect and spirituality—as it encourages others to *"Be Great; Do Great things"*.

Snapshots: Aquarius Suns

Geena Davis
01/21/1956, 00:06 A.M.
Wareham Center, MA

Aquarius Sun: Geena's film career began with the offbeat *"Tootsie"* and her successes came rapidly with *"The Fly"*, *"Beetlejuice"* and *"The Accidental Tourist"* (a film where she played a batty, enthusiastic dog trainer). Three years later, she topped all this with her stellar performance in the rebellious *"Thelma and Louise"*. This flair for eccentric roles is what we'd expect from Aquarius.

Davis displays Aquarius' cubical skull, cheekbones, and jaw—and the square box on the tip of her nose. Once again, we see those sparkling and heavy-lidded eyes, that seem to be focused on a far distant point in space.

Geena's **Aquarius Sun** forms a Grand Square to her **Taurus Moon**, her **27° Libra Ascendant** and **Uranus**. All are on the cross in here chart. Uranus on the Midheaven accounts for her quirky public image, and it empowers her intuitive abilities. It may also be why she's a member of MENSA, the club for geniuses.

Libra Ascendant: Geena's **Ascendant** conjoins Neptune--and they form a trine to Venus, the ruler of her Ascendant and Moon-- and also a sextile to her Pluto/Jupiter conjunction in her 10th House. In addition, Davis' Mars conjoins Saturn and they form a T-square to her Venus and that Jupiter/Pluto conjunction in her 10th House. These powerful aspects give Geena her exceptional athletic skills. She was a semifinalist on the US Olympic Archery Team.

Taurus Moon: Geena's Fixed Earth Moon also trines that 10th House Jupiter/Pluto conjunction, and it also sextiles her Venus. With this, Geena tends to express her emotions in a calm and well controlled manner.

Notably—save for her Mercury—all of Davis' components have seven major aspects to other components. This likely accounts for her unique personality and her powerful physicality and intuitive abilities.

Paul Newman
Jan. 26, 1925, 6:30 A.M.,
Cleveland, Ohio

Aquarius Sun: Paul's top photos reveal a common Aquarius trait, that all-knowing, externally focused look in the eyes. At times, this look can be unsettling, particularly when you're having a personal talk with one of your Aquarius friends, and his or her aloof mannerisms leave the impression that "you're not even there".

This "look" is due to Aquarius' inflated and angled eyelids, that appear to be focusing on some point in outer space, rather than on what's in front of them. Or it might be that their brains are always tuning into concepts, far different than the one currently being discussed. Watch closely, and watch how they constantly check the incoming flow of others into the room—and then abruptly end the conversation—to skip away to greet another newly arrived friend. You'll be left there standing alone, feeling lost in the crowd. To find some sympathy, seek out a Water Sign.

In his two biggest box office successes: *"The Sting"* and *"Butch Cassidy"*, Newman presented Aquarius' idealized sense of optimism. In his roles in *Hud"* and *"Cool Hand Luke"*, we saw the distant demeanor of his Sun, as well as his chilly Capricorn Ascendant. In *"Cat on A Hot Tin Roof"*, even Liz Taylor (with her intense Scorpio Moon) could not illicit any emotion from her alienated lover.

Capricorn Ascendant: Mercury, Venus and Jupiter conjoin Paul's earthy Capricorn Ascendant. This is why, when he attempts to express his ideas to others, his voice becomes deep and grounded. Physically, this Rising Sign gives him the broad, high-placed cheekbones and the caverns under his eyes. What we see is the somber appearance of a goat.

Like *Leonardo DiCaprio*, Paul has Saturn on his Midheaven. His highest reward also came late in his career. After seven Oscar nominations, he finally received his first Oscar win in 1987, as *Best Actor* for his role in *"Color of Money"*.

Pisces Moon: In many roles, Paul played characters, who constantly questioned their actions. This vulnerability undercut his machismo image, but it added depth and enriched the quality of his performances. This sensitive side was brought to light by his **Pisces Moon**. This lunar compassion showed in his charity, where (with his Pisces wife *Joanne Woodward*), they fulfilled their desire to create a camp for ill children. The profits from *"Newman's Own"* food products continue to support this charity, many years after his passing.

Snapshots: Pisces Suns

"Miracles happen everyday. Change your perception of what is a miracle, and you'll see them all around you" **Jon Bon Jovi**

Jon Bon Jovi
3/2/1962, 8:45 p.m.,
Perth Amboy, NJ

Pisces Sun: With his Pisces Sun trine its ruling planet Neptune, Jon was given a gift for music. With his Cardinal components, he was given the drive to make his dreams a reality! After Jovi's initial success in "grunge music" faded in 1993, this hard-working Pisces Jon created the score for *"Young Guns II"*. His tune *"Blaze of Glory"* was in that film and it became his first #1 hit.

With age, Bon Jovi continued to adapt, as he learned to express his thoughts on his faith in human potential—a quality given to him by his Saturn, Mercury, Mars and Jupiter in Aquarius. This was apparent in his uplifting anthem *"It's My Life"*. It encourages "all to live life to the fullest".

Jon shows the physical traits of Pisces. Most noticeable are the thick-lidded and watery "fish eyes". Note how his one eye floats high above the other, and how his nose and mouth skew to the left—while his the chin angles to the right. With Mutable Signs, nothing runs in a straight line.

Libra Ascendant: With Libra rising, Bon Jovi presents the pleasant mask, that clearly depicts his public personae. He is not the typical "in your face" rock star—he's likeable! Perhaps that's why, in 1996, *People Magazine* named him one of the world's 50 most beautiful people. Physically, Jon's Libra traits include the wide V-shaped smile with the cherub dimples. When Libra rises, his deep-pooled eyes lit up, as Libra's cardinal energy straightens his Pisces' skewed solar features into horizontal lines.

Capricorn Moon: With his Moon in Capricorn, Jon is emotionally driven to work hard, excel and make his mark on society! In 2004, he campaigned for John Kerry, purchased co-ownership in an AFL Football franchise and finished a new album. In 2006, he took on his first title role in *"National Lampoon's The Trouble with Frank"*. Through all this, he brags that his 16 year relationship with his wife is monogamous. The material nature of this Earthy Moon shows in his quote: "The only thing I like more than my wife is my money".

In this ending, Drew Barrymore shows us how the *"transitions in a person's life"* are defined by his or her three key components. Drew's life give us hints of what to observe, as we watch the children (and grand-children) in our lives—and how they grow into being adults.

Drew Barrymore
2/22/1975, 11:51 A.M.
Culver City, CA

Moon in Cancer, Childhood: From birth to 8 years of age, children have few shields and little self identity. A child's initial response is to "react emotionally" to their worlds—"Ouch, stove hot!" This period reflects the *qualities of a child's Moon*.

At six years old, Drew won world fame with her role in the movie *E.T.* There, she "moved our emotions", as her *mothering Cancer Moon* kept the little alien out of harm's way. With natal Saturn joining her sensitive Water Moon and Mars in opposition, her sudden stardom resulted in a notoriously troubled childhood. At age 9, Drew began drinking alcohol. At age 12, she was addicted to cocaine, and a year later she entered rehabilitation. After earning the title of the *Wild Child of Hollywood*, it was now time for her to make some major changes in her life.

Ascendant in Gemini, Adolescence: With their learned lunar memories and instincts, the next step in personal growth comes, when people enter their teens. Here, *they become obsessed with how they appear to others.*

In this phase in her life, Drew's public mask constantly changed, as her Gemini persona took on different roles in films that ranged from horror, comedy to pre-teen angst. At the age of 15, this inspired her to write her 1st book: *"Little Girl Lost"*.

Sun in Pisces, Adulthood: At age 23, in her role in the 1998 Cinderella fable *Ever After,* Drew's **Pisces Sun** finally found "the peace within", as she began to portray characters, who suffered greatly but still found goodness in other people. Her friends maintain that Drew was very happy at this stage in her life. Astrologers would say that she has found **the purpose of her Pisces Sun** for, and at this time, she was more able to connect with (and express) her feelings to others. As of 2021, Drew has written 4 books and formed a successful film and TV production company. Yes, her dreams came true!

In Finale:

If there was nothing to see in Astrology, it would not have piqued the interest of millions of people around the world for thousands of years!

Why do those "who have studied astrology" instantly understand the dialogue of other astrologers, even though they have never met? This is because **astrology works for all of those, who have learned the language of this ancient art.**

Even with recent scientific discoveries like *Quantum Entanglement*, many scientists remain skeptical about astrology. This is because they have not viewed the evidence, or attempted to understand this artful language. If they did, they would realize that astrology's macro-view of the Universe parallels the arrangements in modern astrophysics. Likewise, the diminishing degrees in astrology's decans and duads are showing us how identical patterns are occurring in the tiniest of arrangements, that have been revealed by particle physicists.

These two scientific disciplines show that this ancient Hermetic proverb is true:
"As above, so below; as below, so above"

Use the Stars to achieve your creative Destiny:

The real value of astrology is that it tells us about ourselves—and the common issues in the "human condition". Astrology's divine operating instructions are the guiding light—that tell individuals of their given gifts, and the steps that they can follow—to achieve their creative purpose in life. These important insights can only be obtained by understanding the art and language of astrology, and the content in one's own astrology chart.

One's moment of birth is significant, but *destiny is not an act of serendipity!* The only one who can keep your life on track—is YOU! With that, this author encourages the reader to explore your personal "heavenly lesson plan", and use it to evaluate your goals and how you can manifest them in your life.

Your life will be enriched by the insights of astrology, but this author does not encourage any one to run their lives by the Stars. In more trying times, you may have to contact a "wise and knowledgeable astrologer" to guide you through the "treacherous currents".

Good luck! The Universe is wishing you to succeed on every one of your adventures, for you are part of the Divine Plan, that is operating everywhere.

Hopefully, this book has helped you to *define the trail* that you will travel down, in the years ahead.

William Schreib, 2022